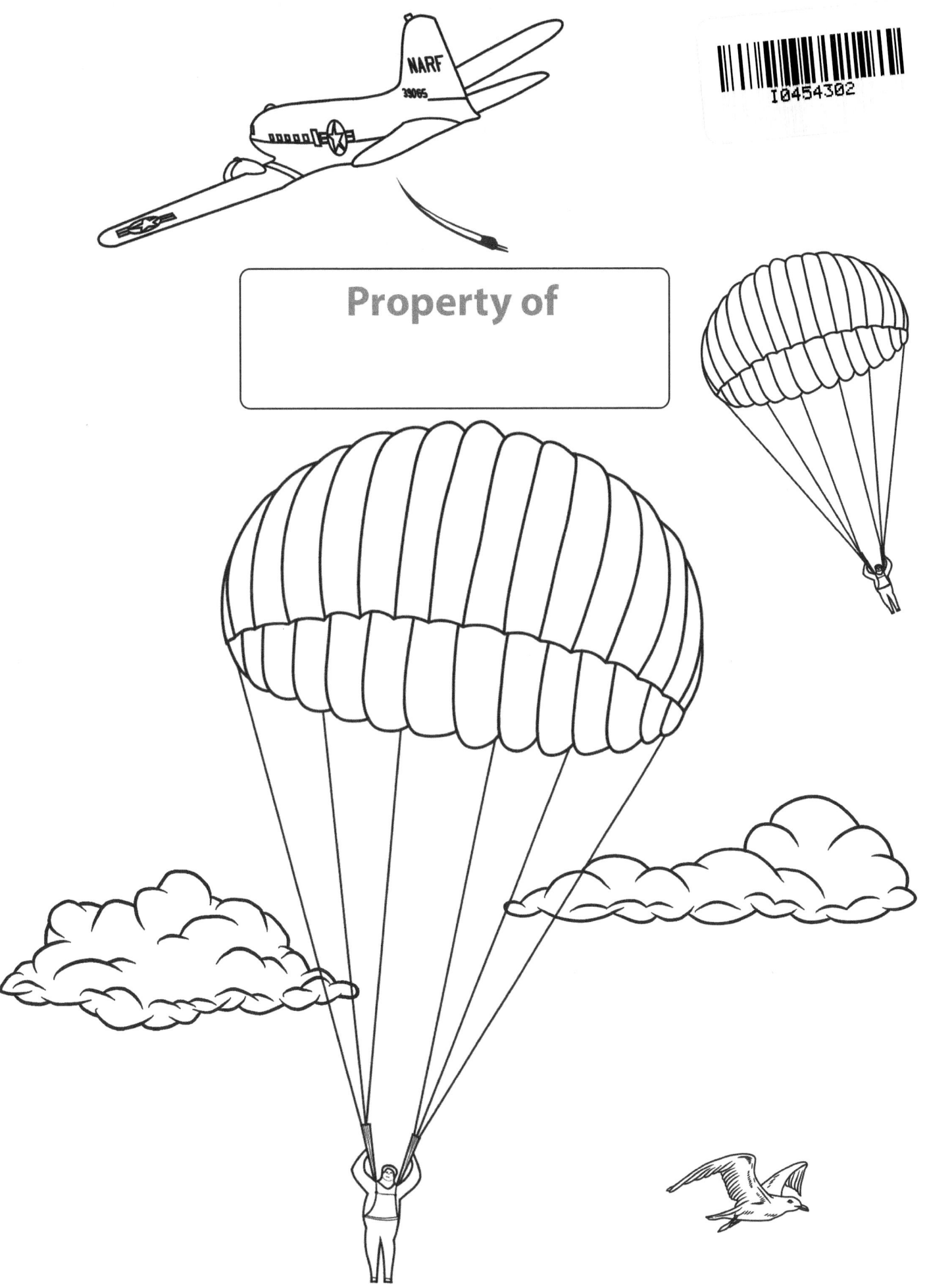

Property of

Amazon Book ASIN B0CNXL918W

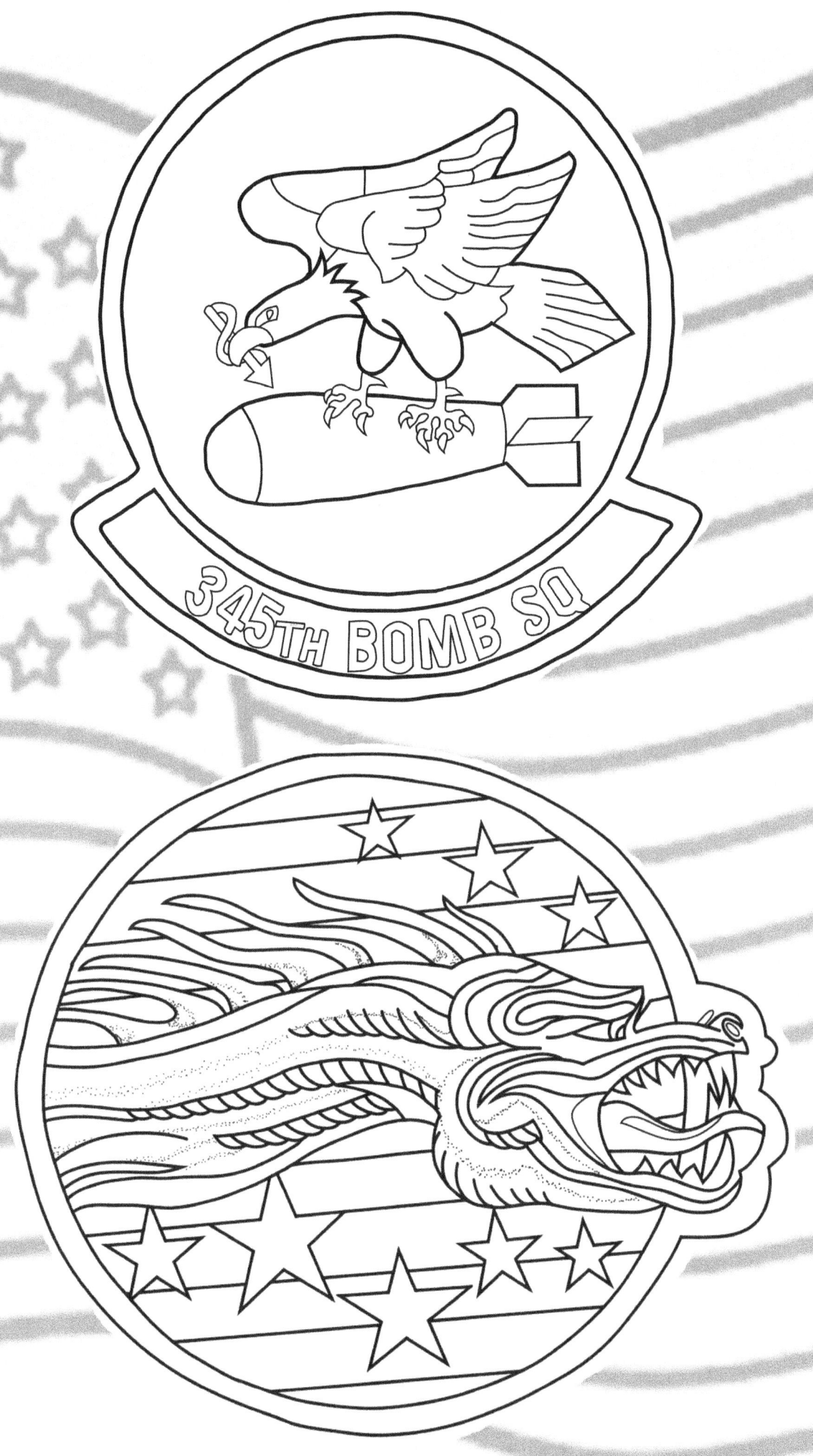

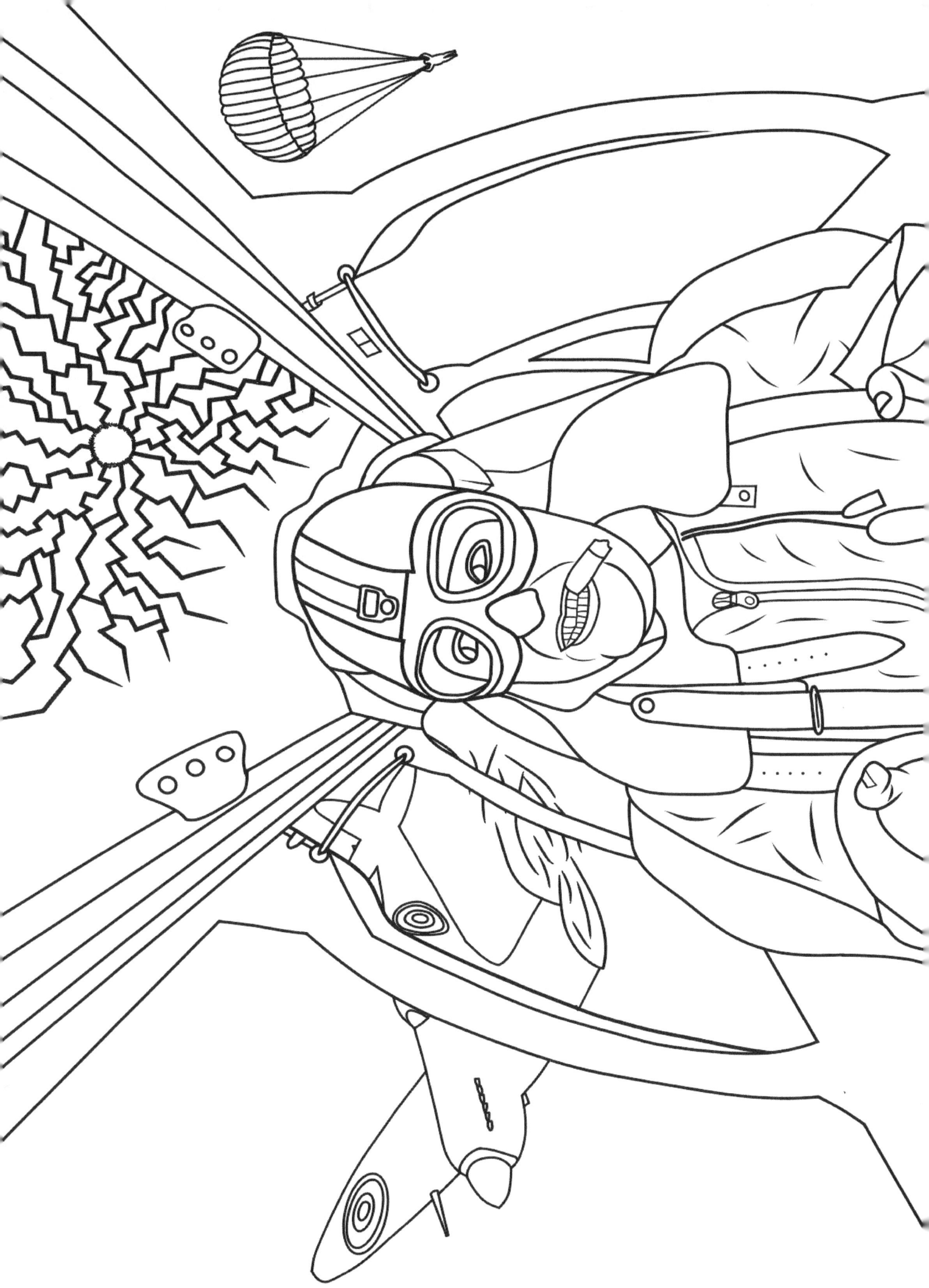

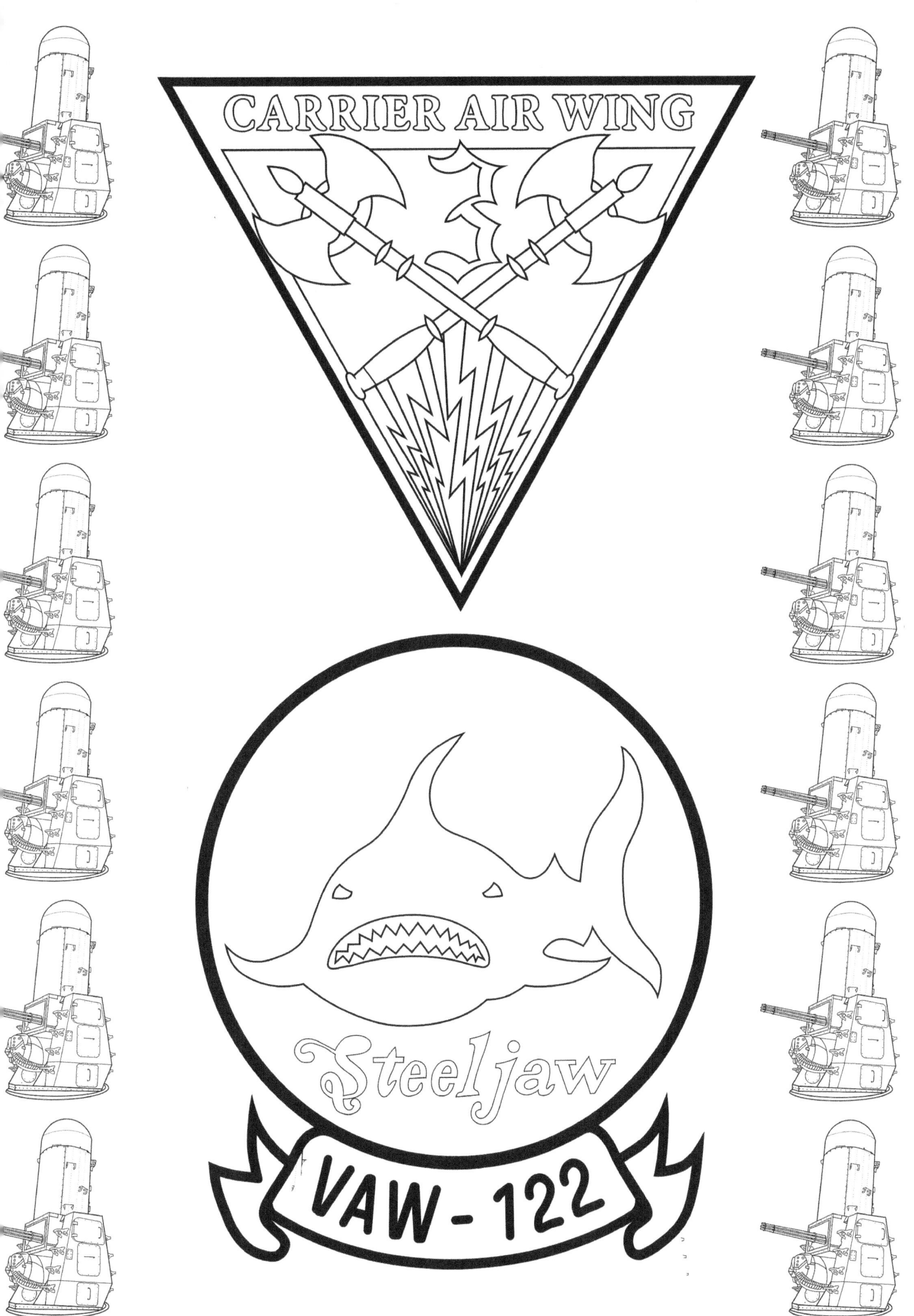

CARRIER AIR WING

Steeljaw

VAW - 122

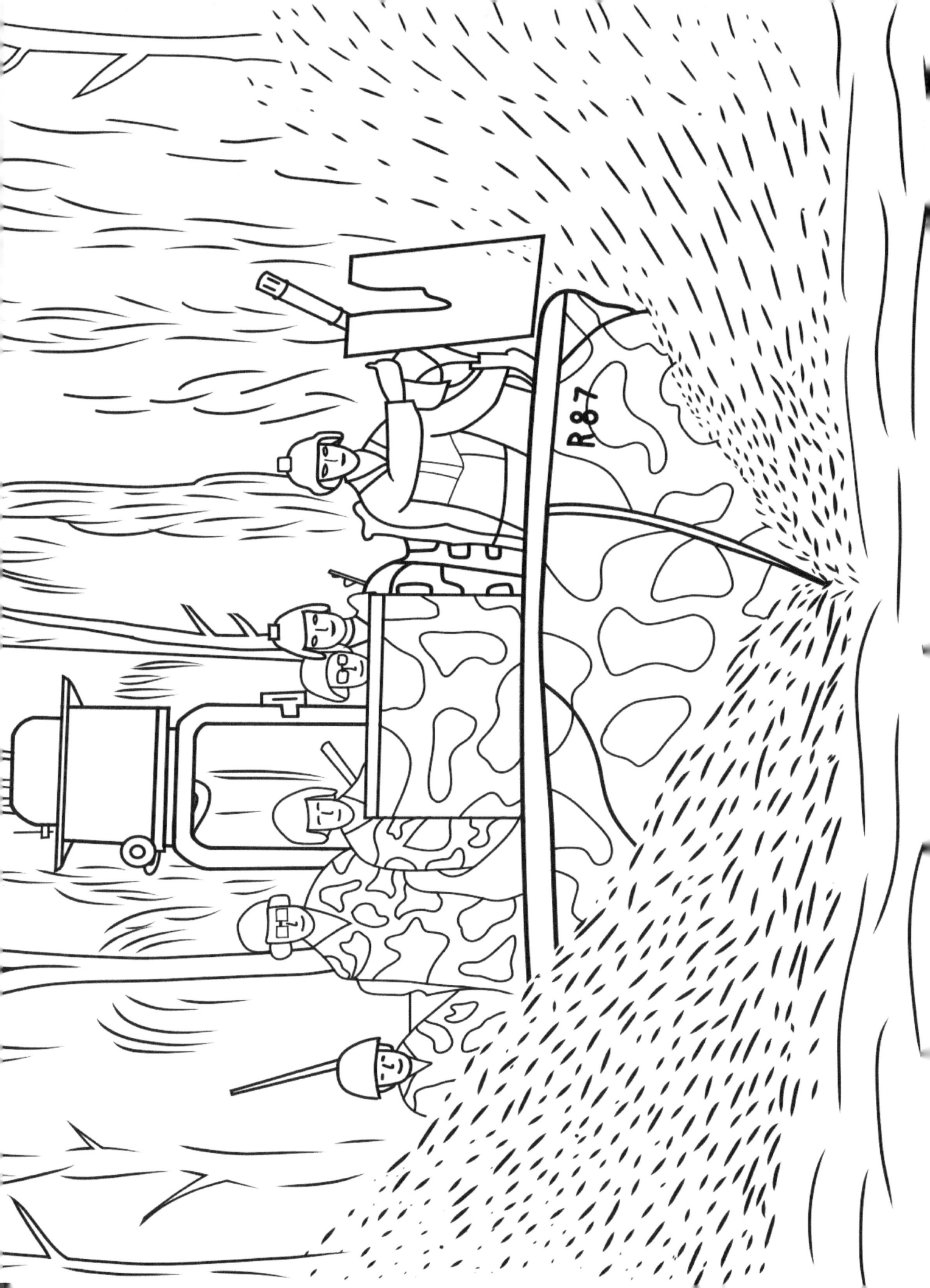

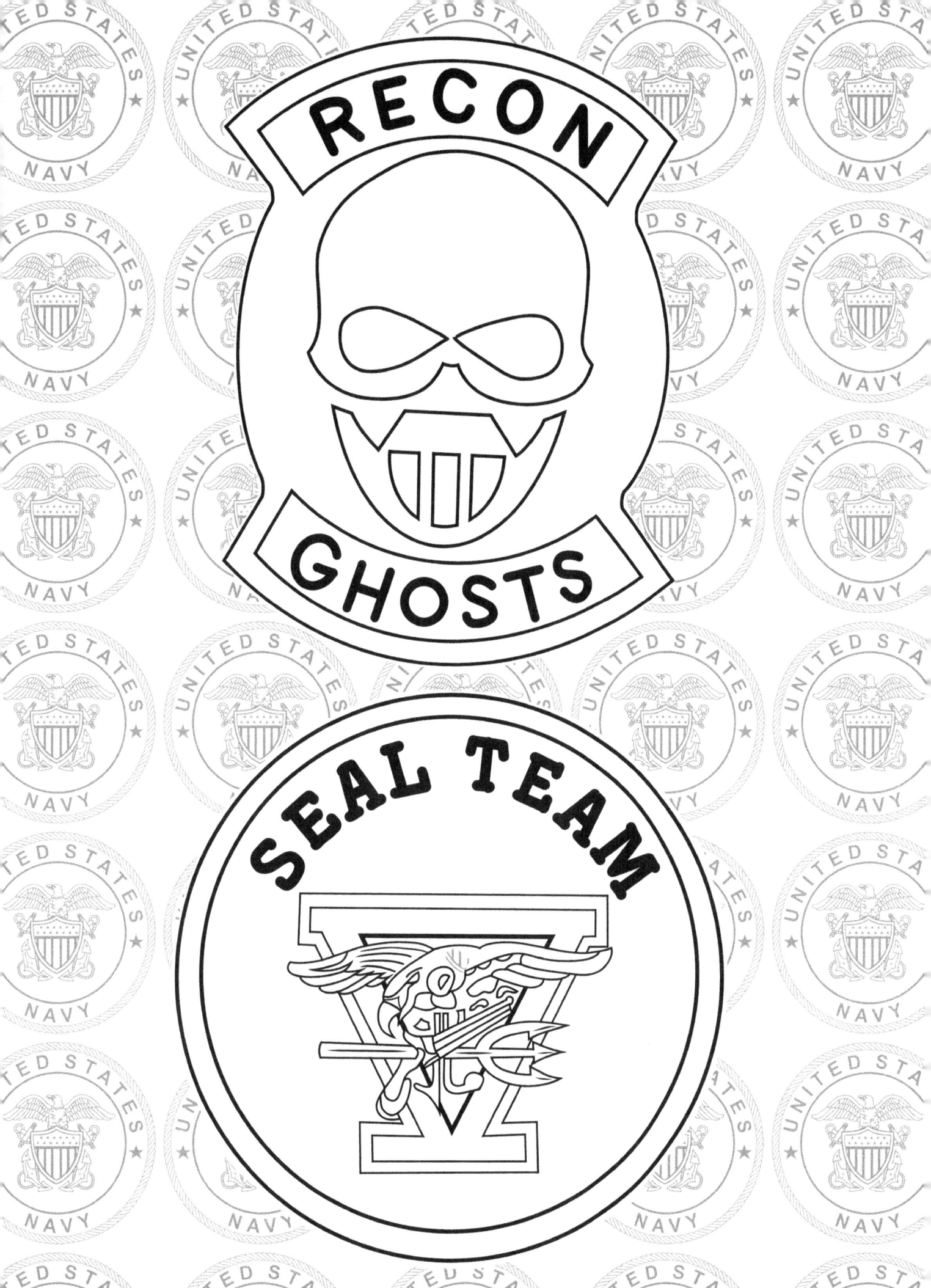

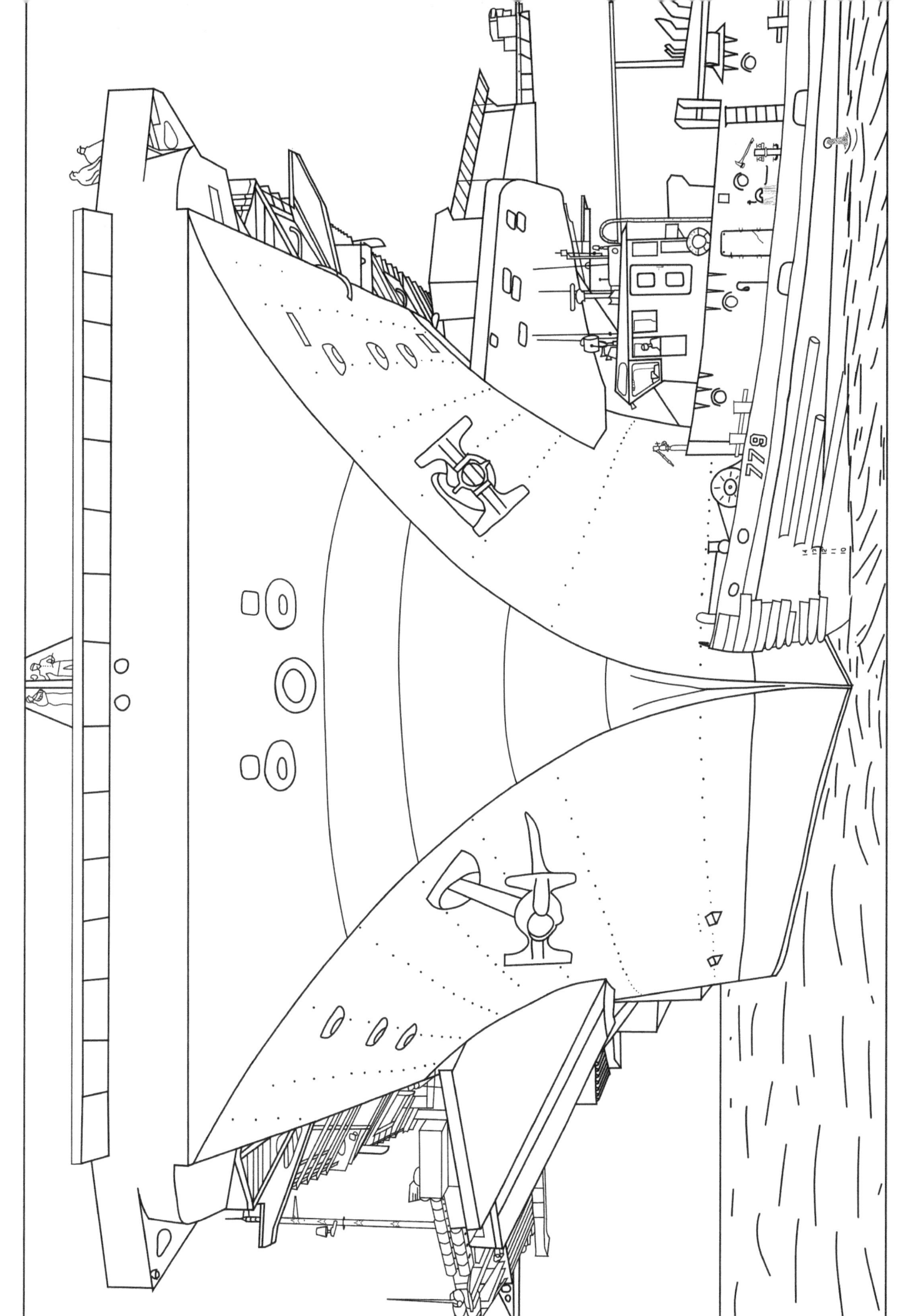

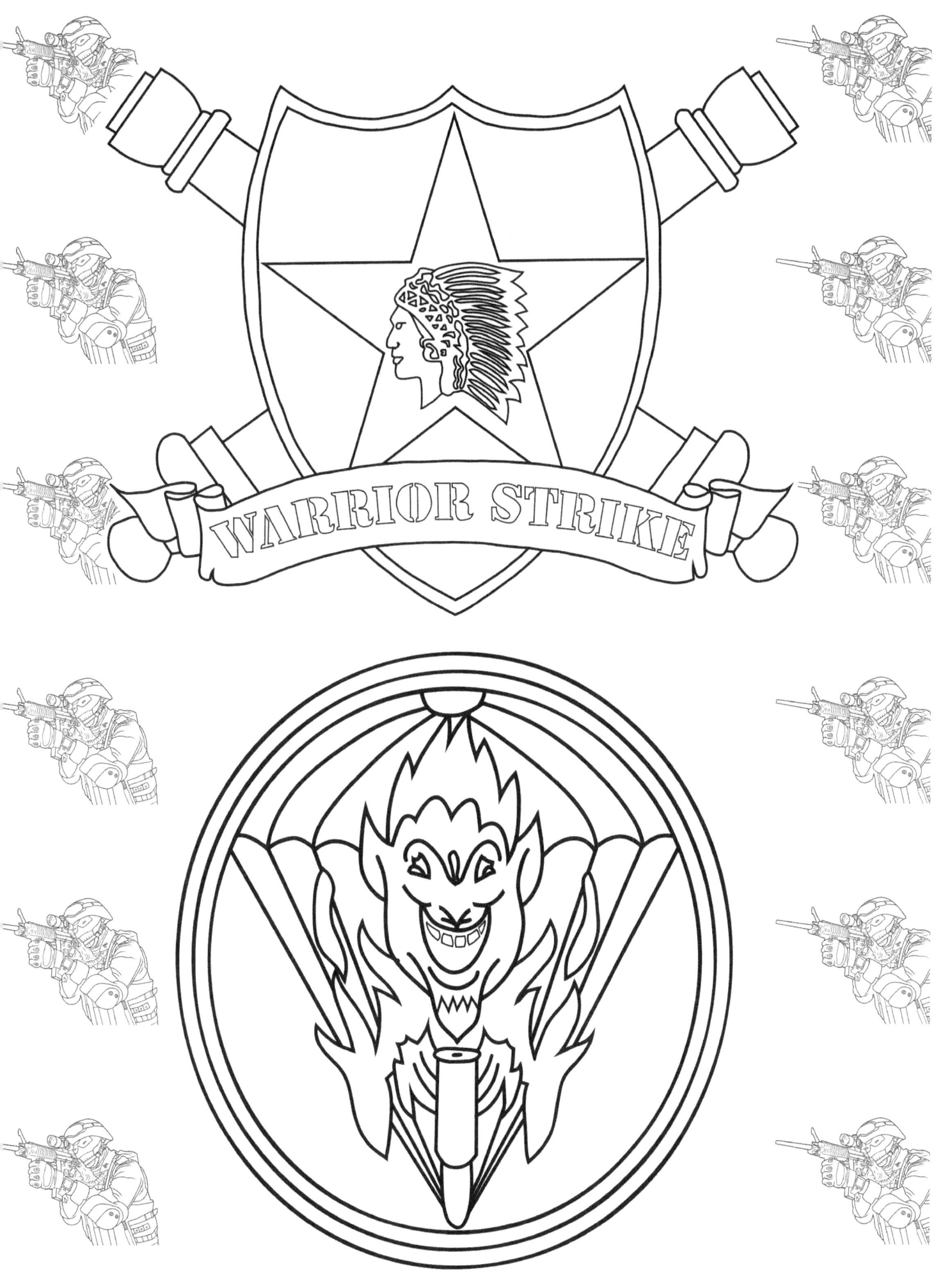

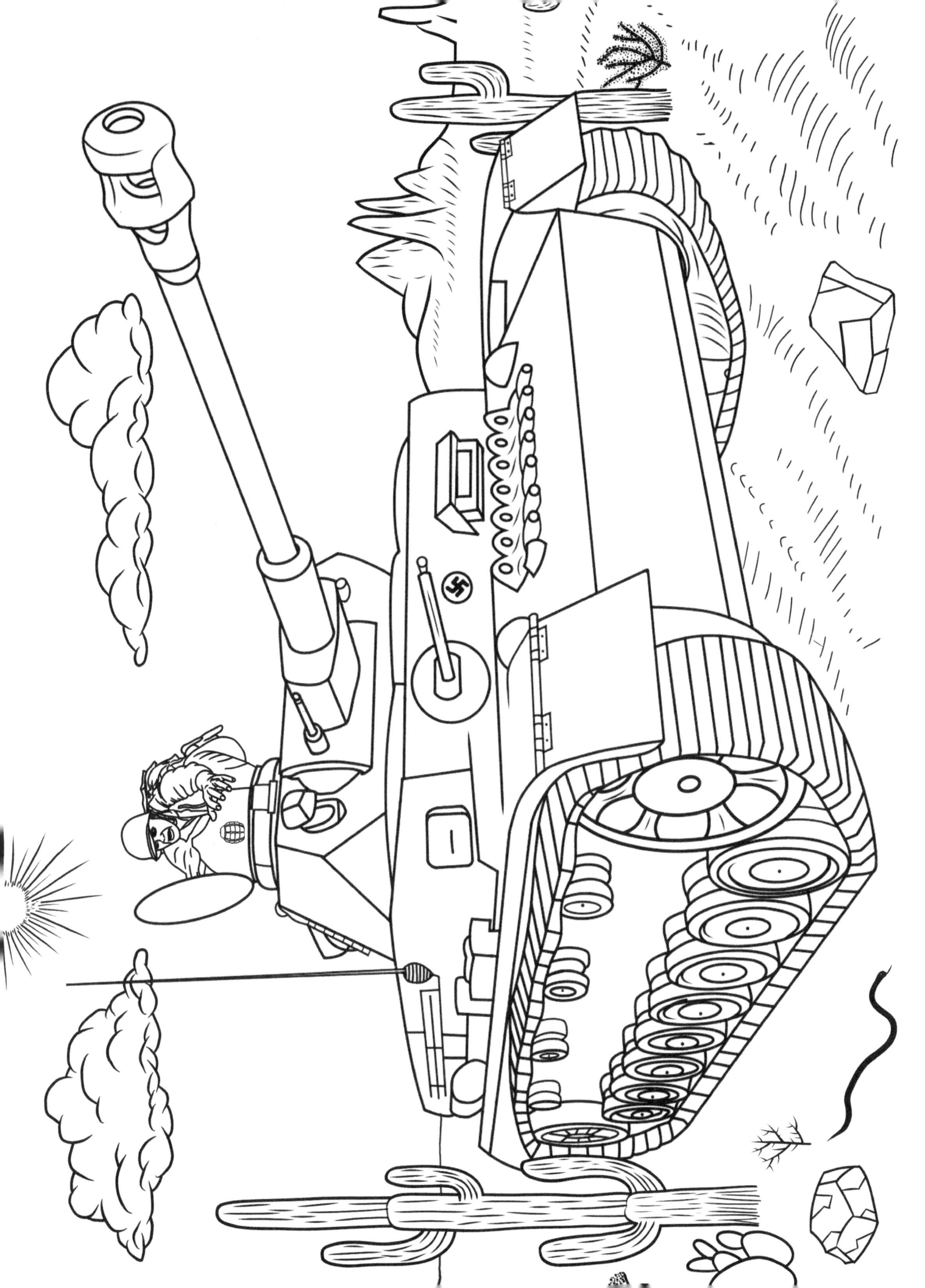

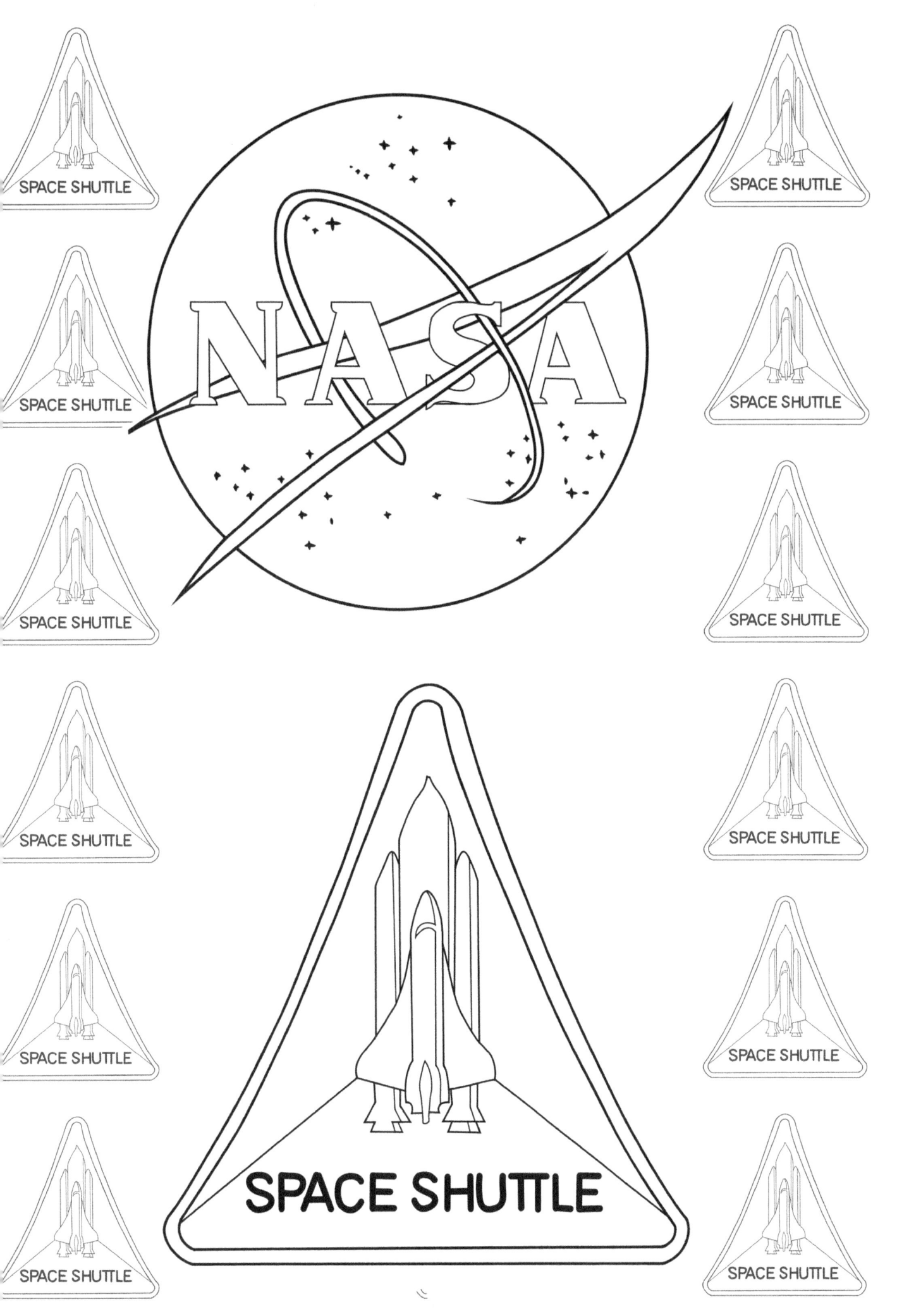

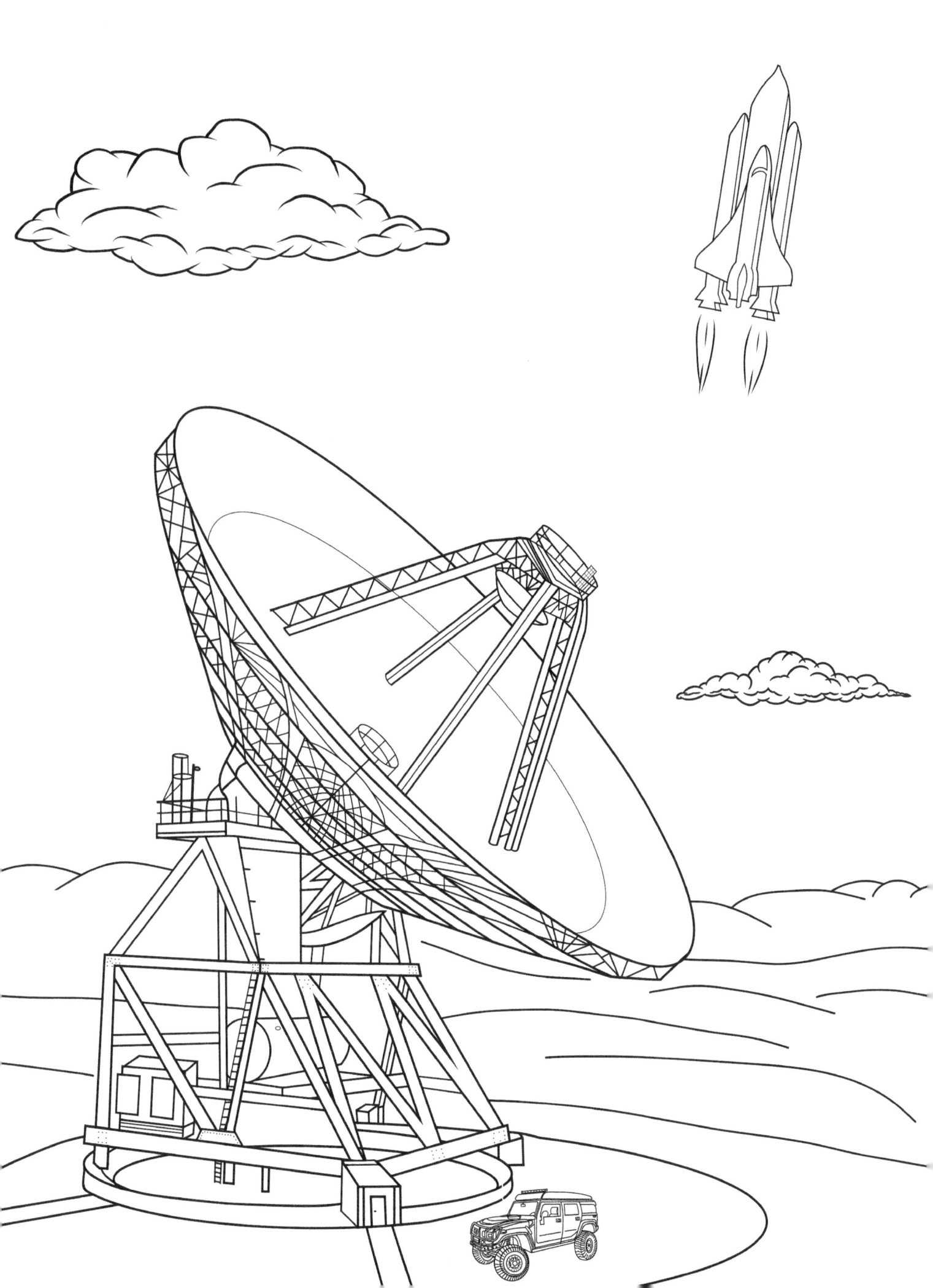

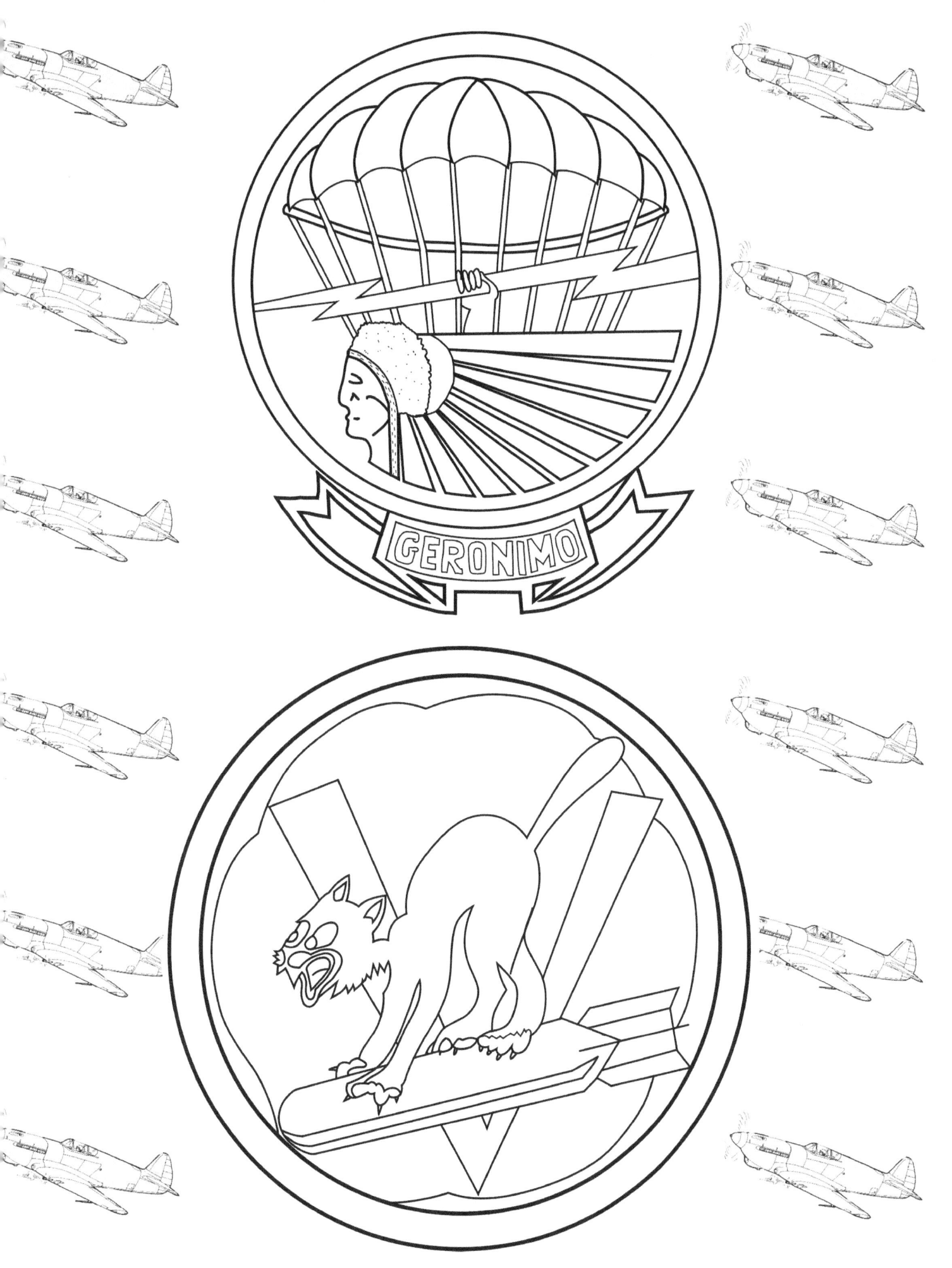

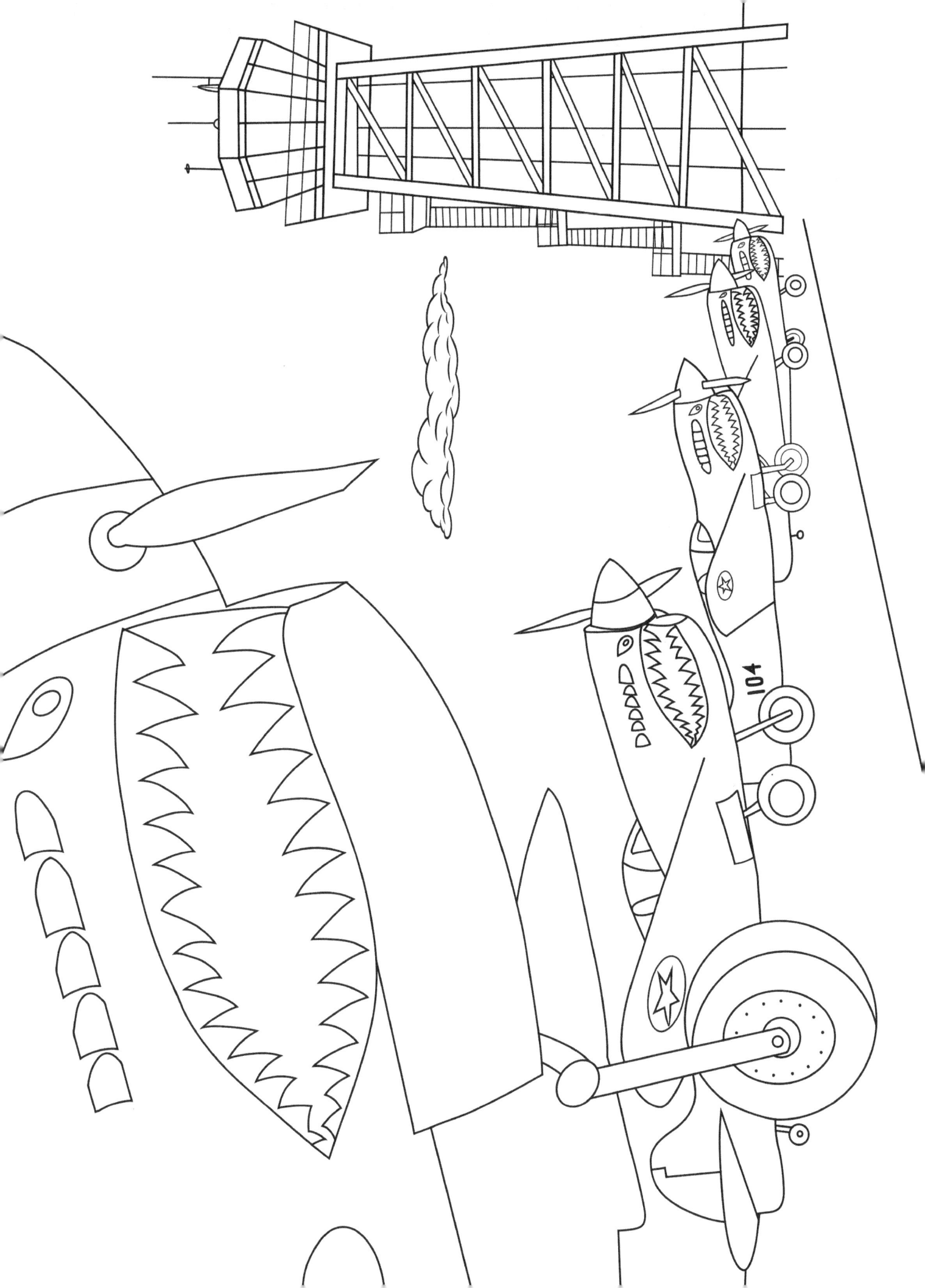

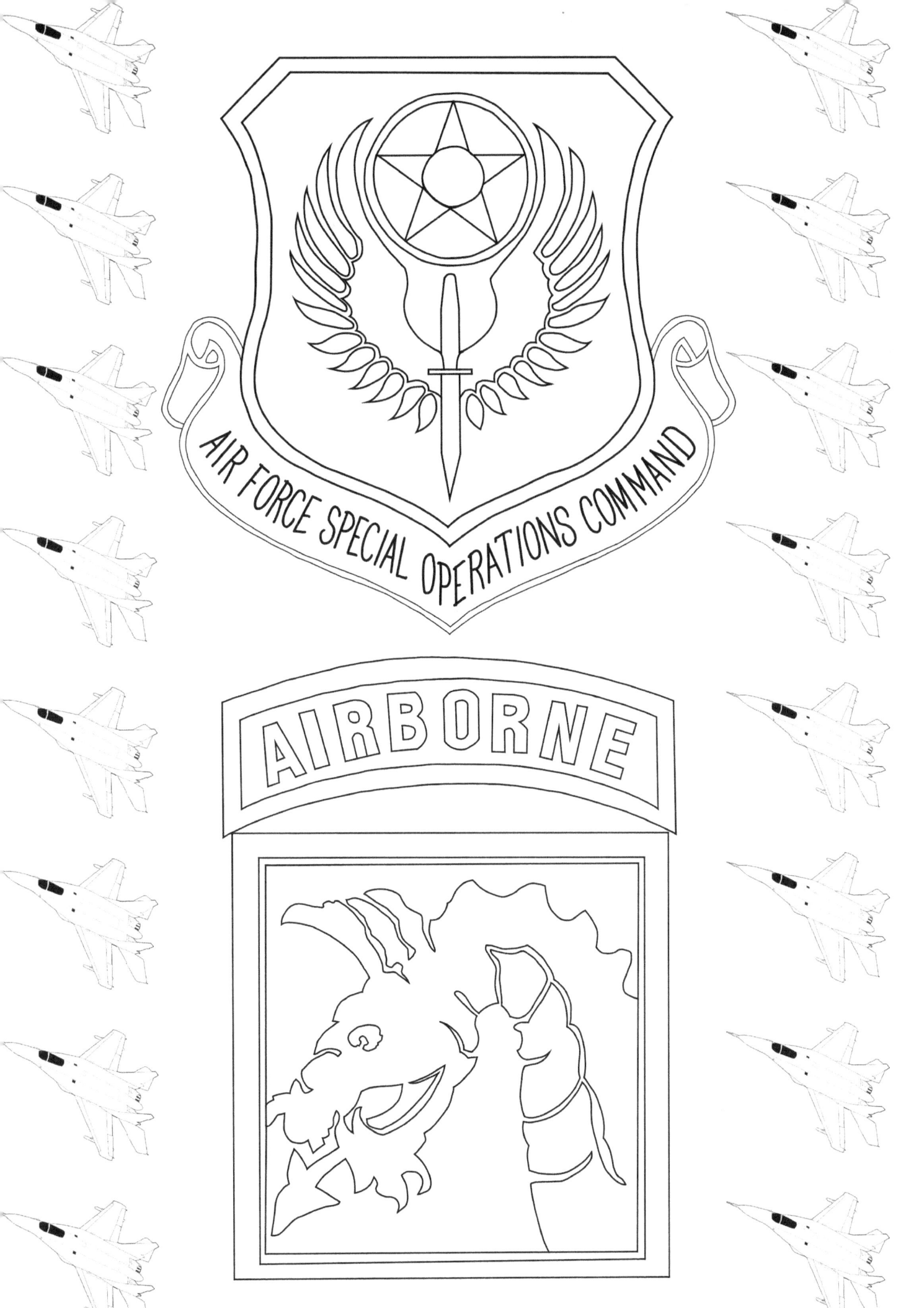

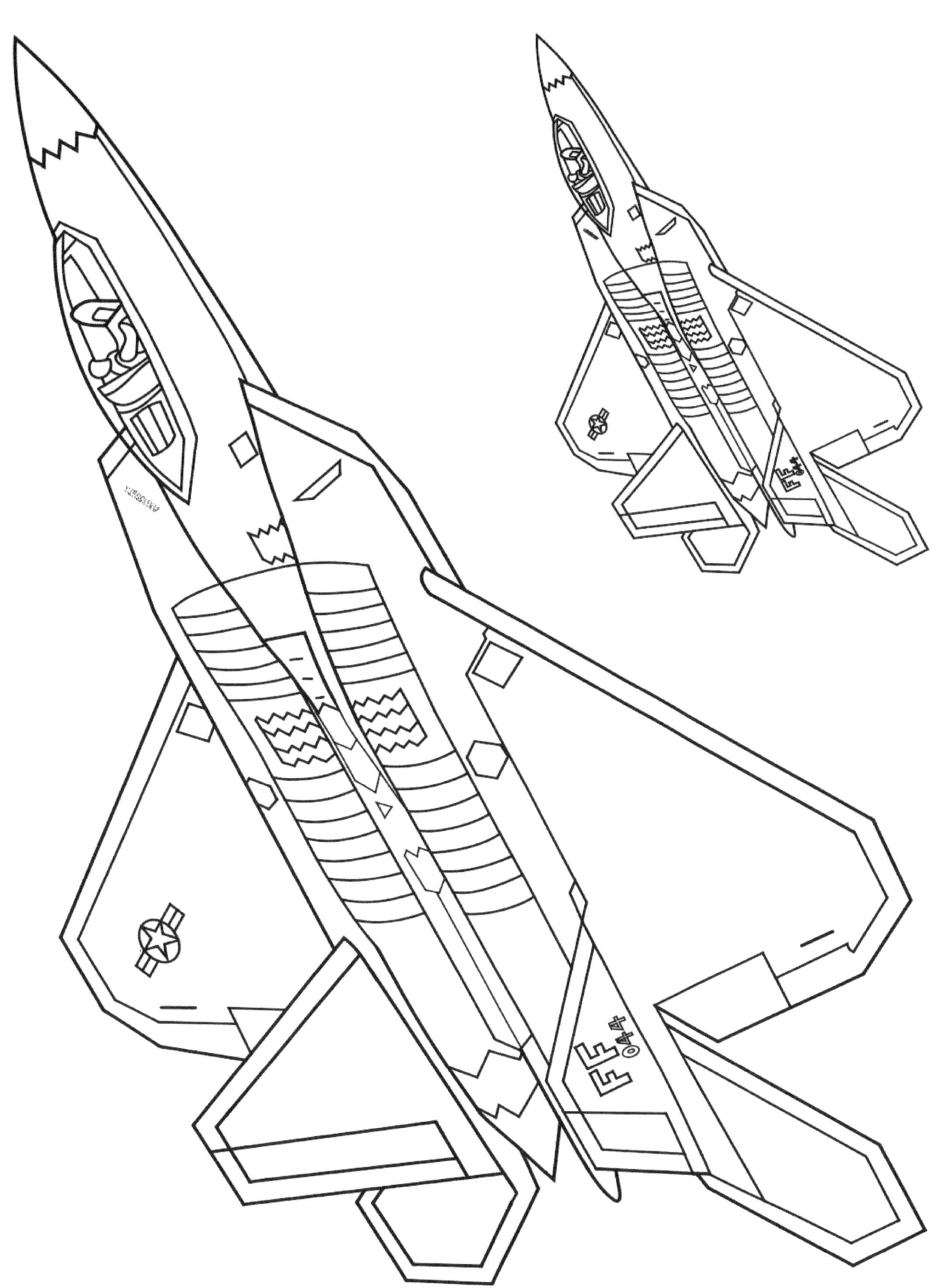

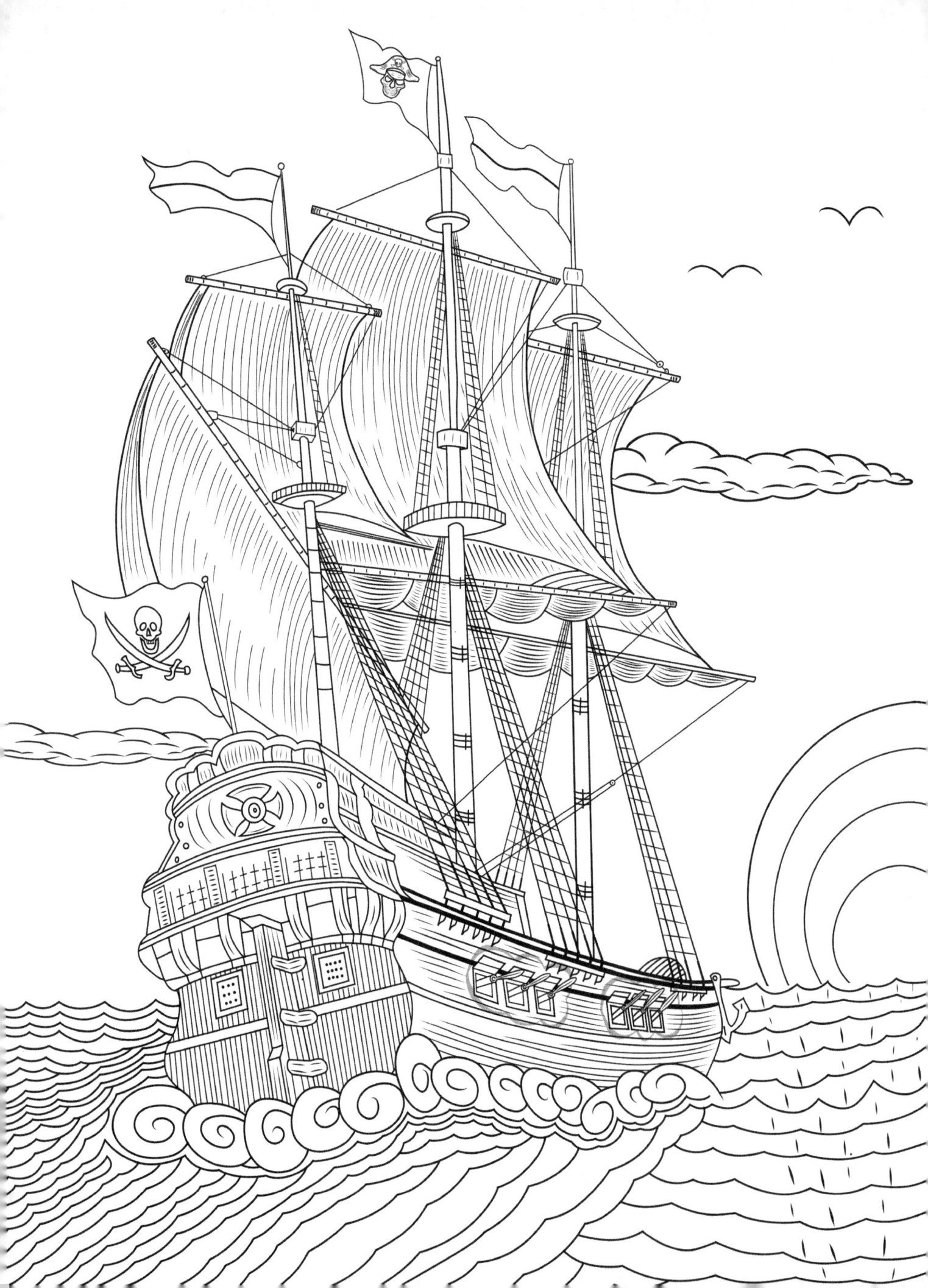

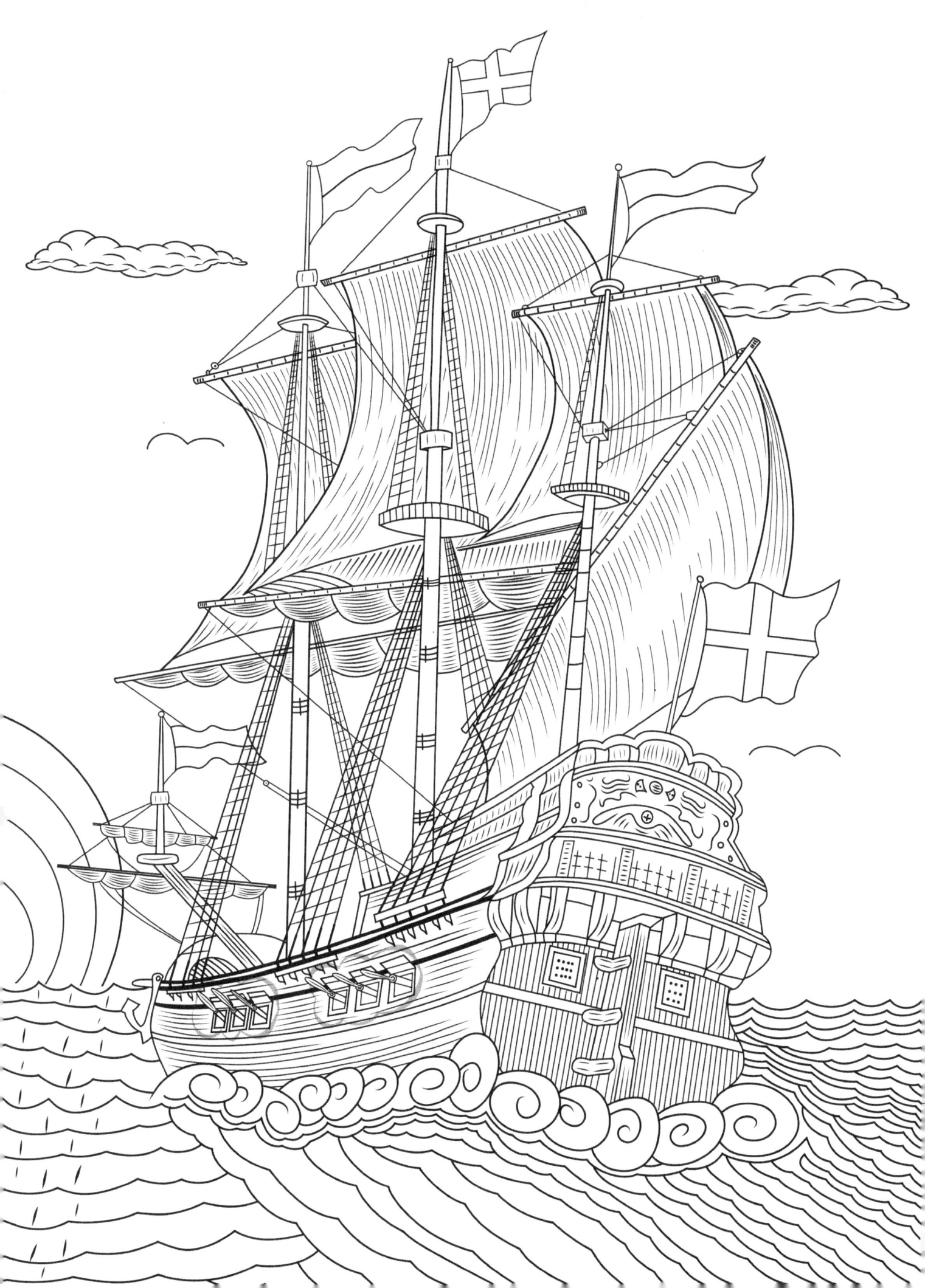

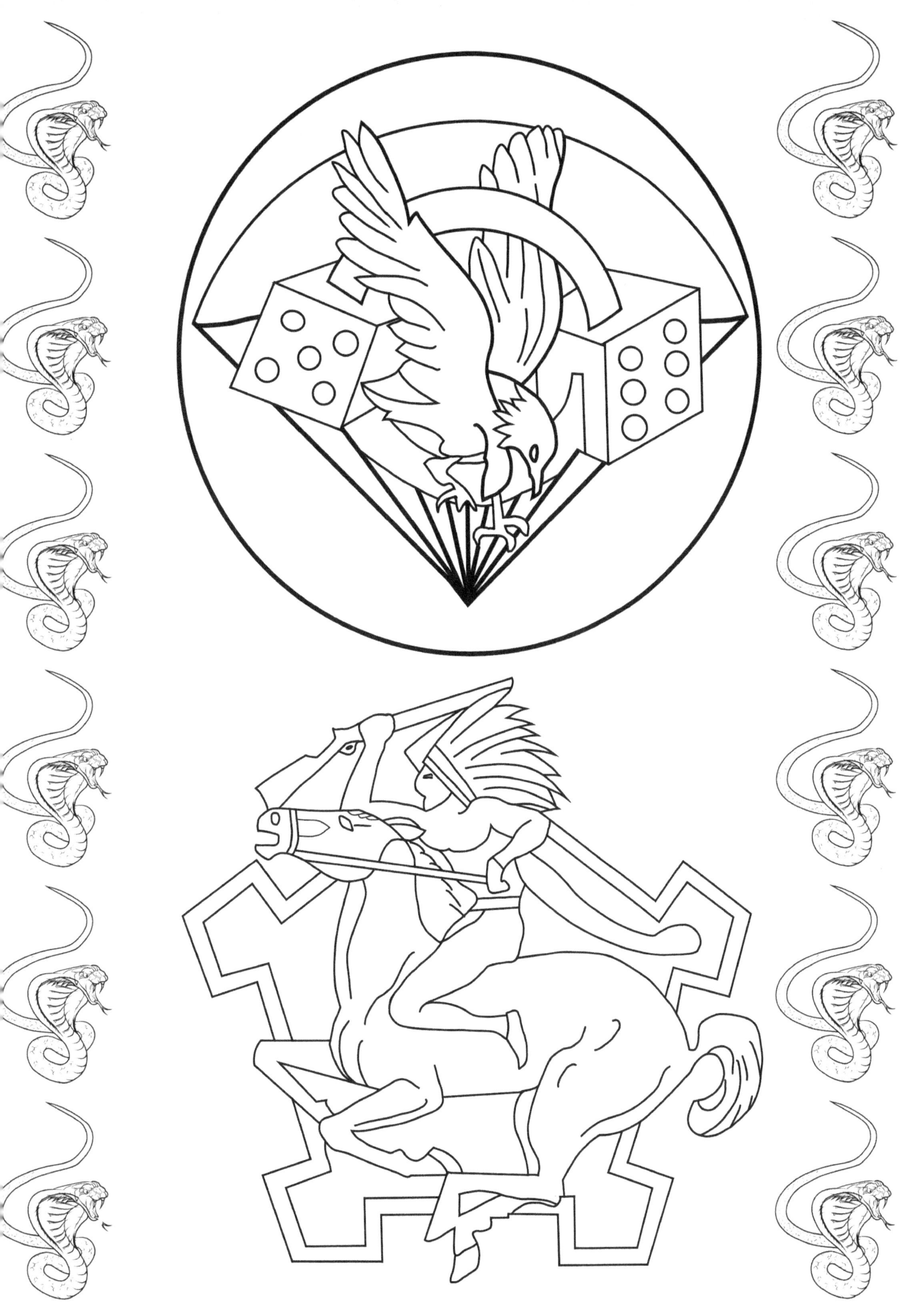

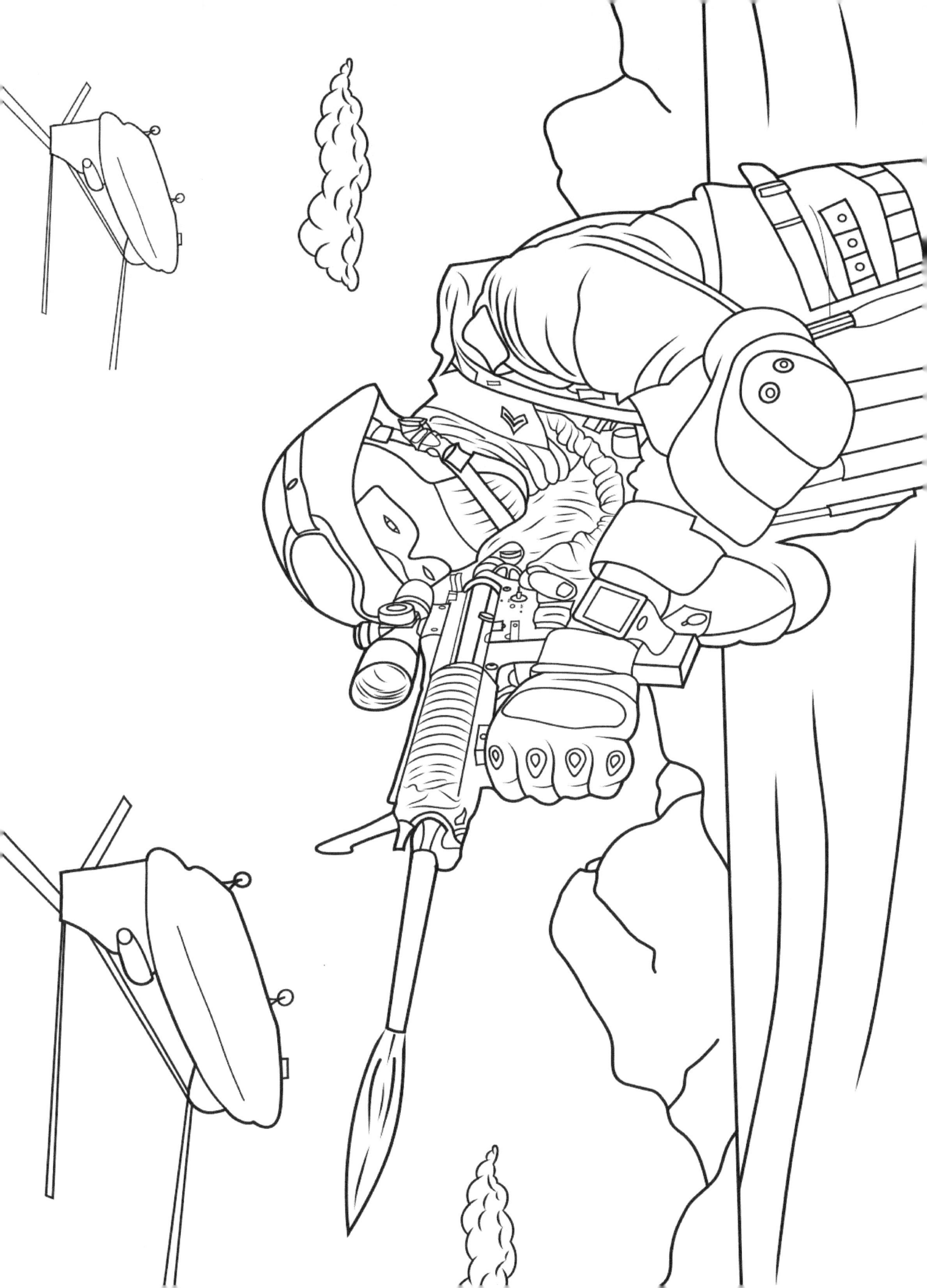

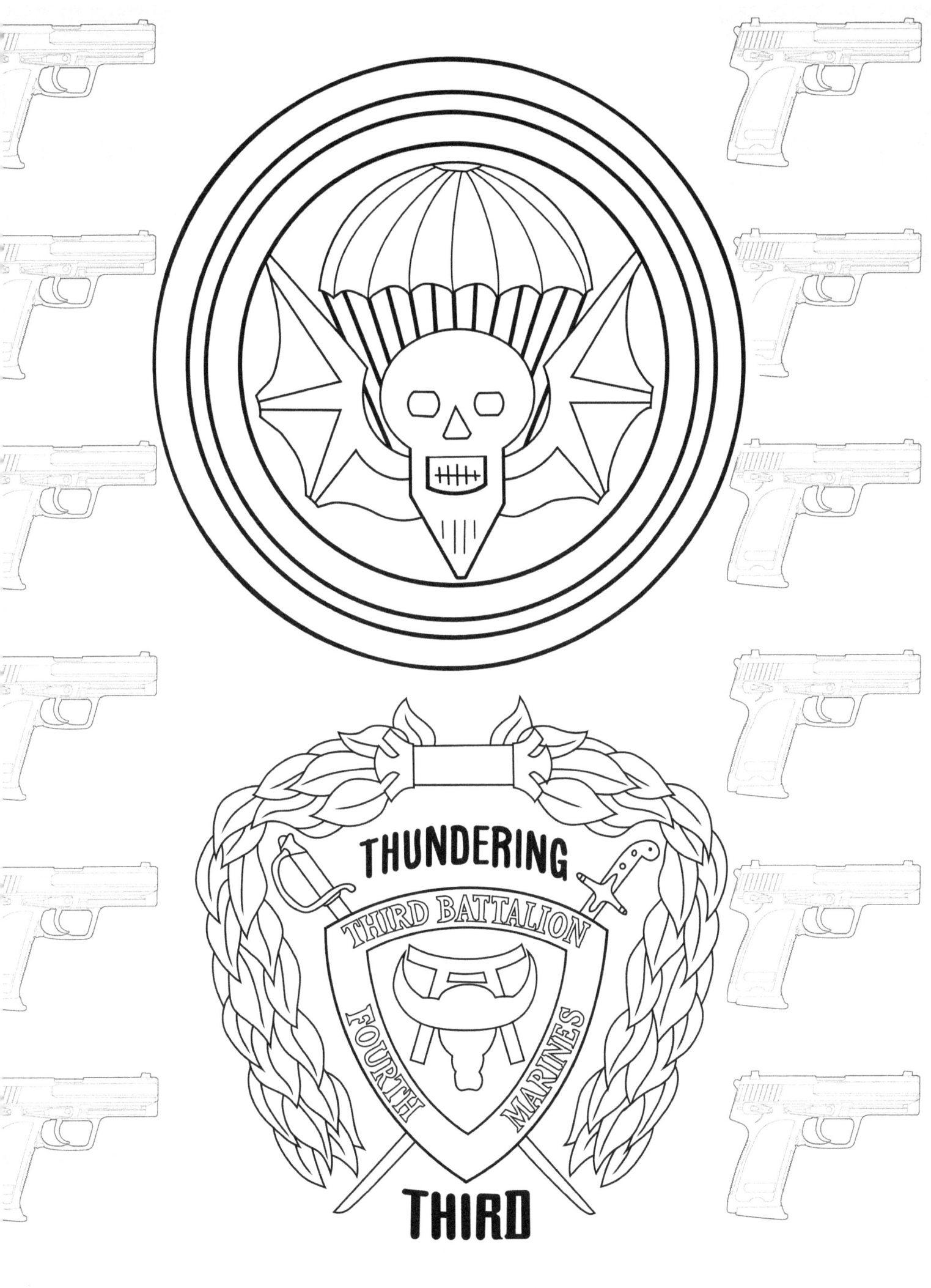

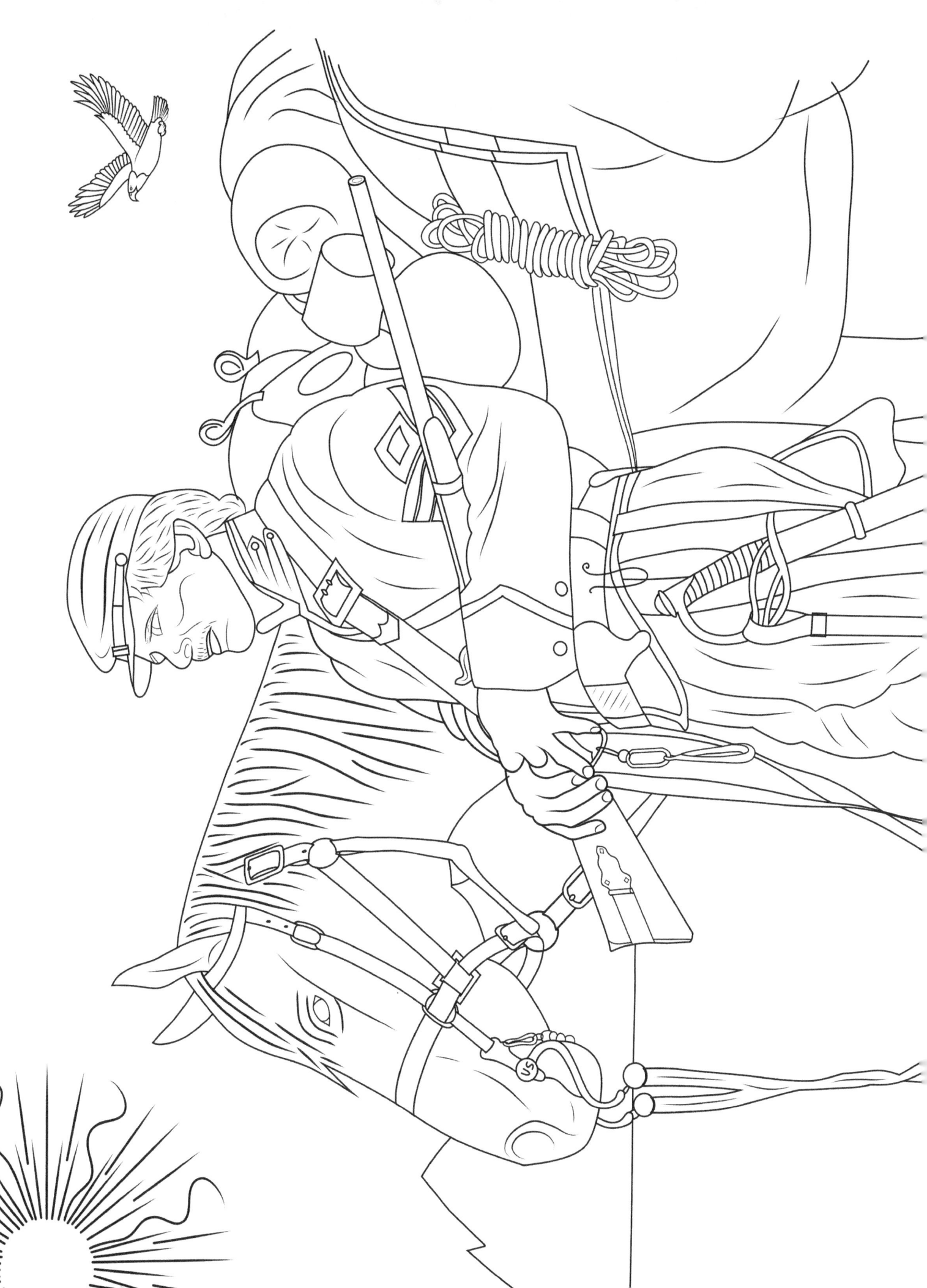

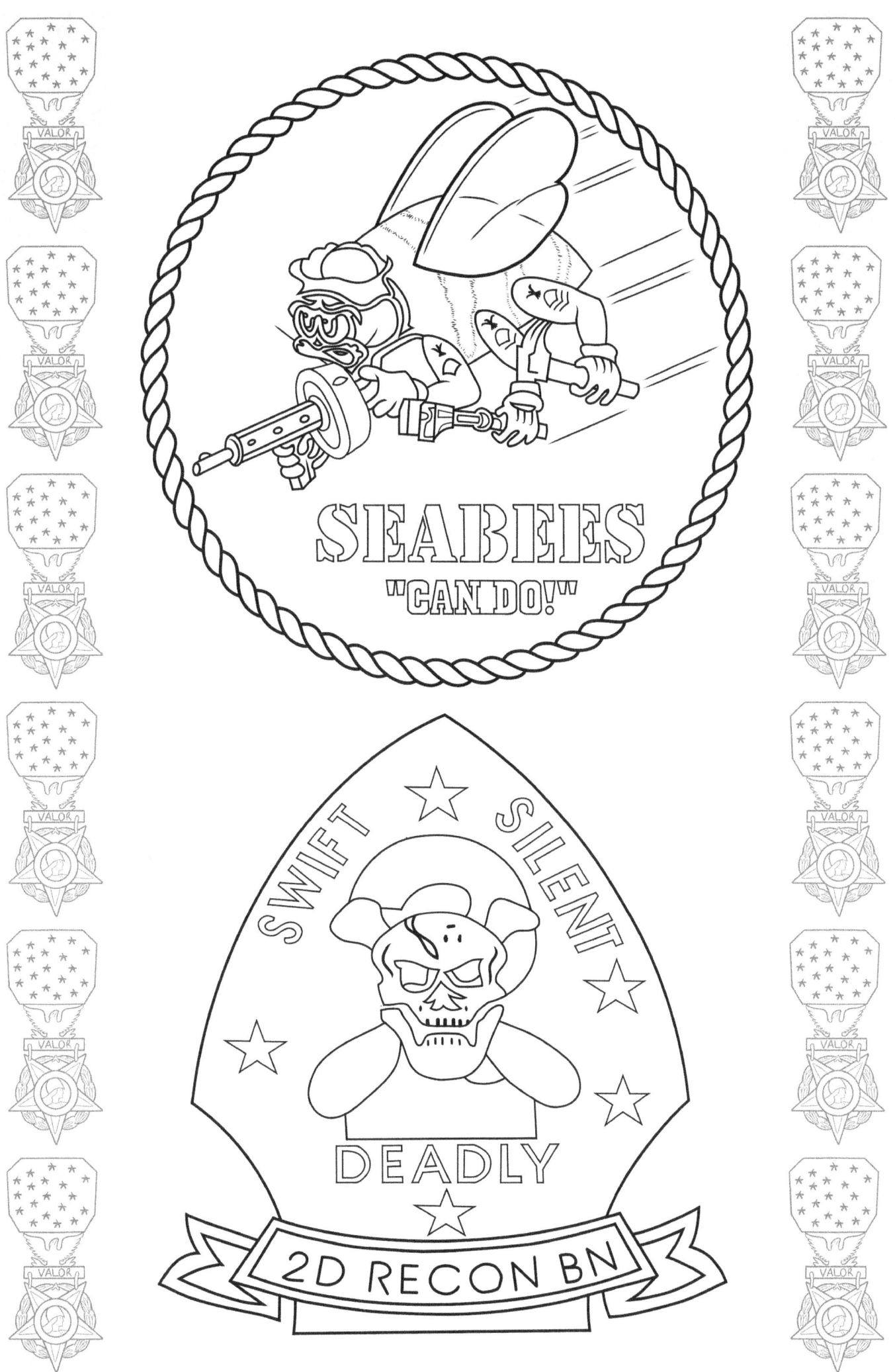

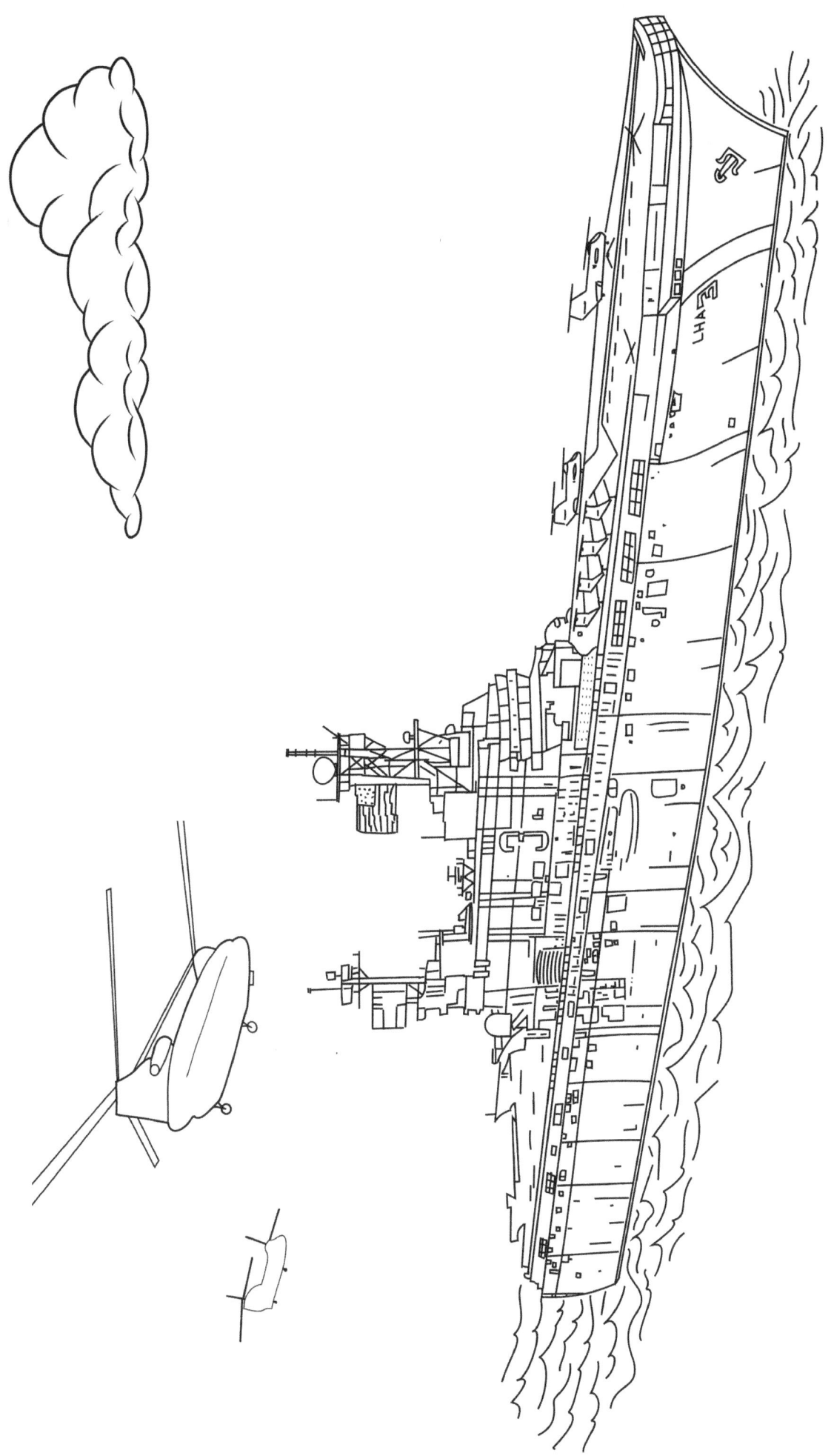

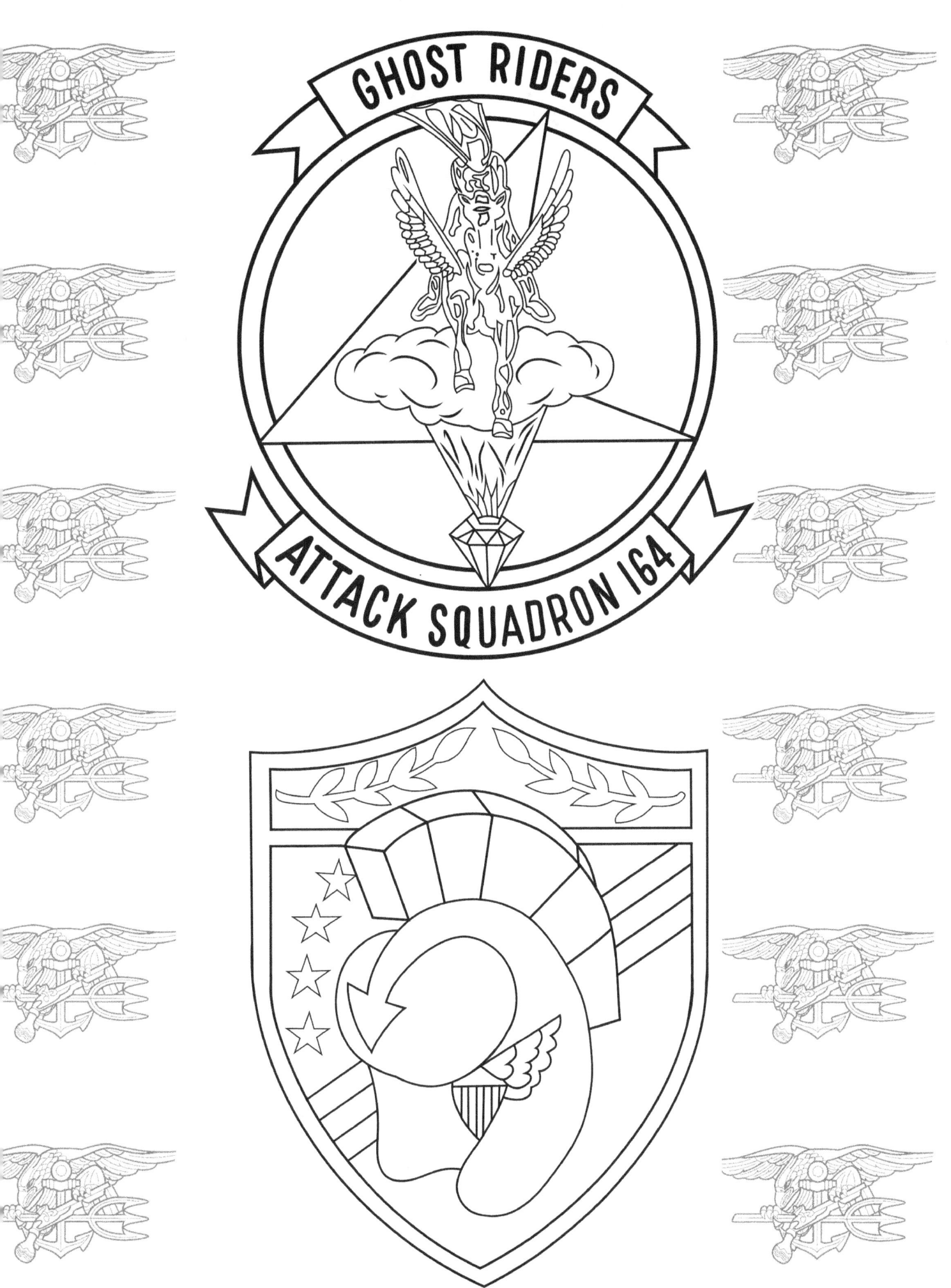

GHOST RIDERS

ATTACK SQUADRON 164

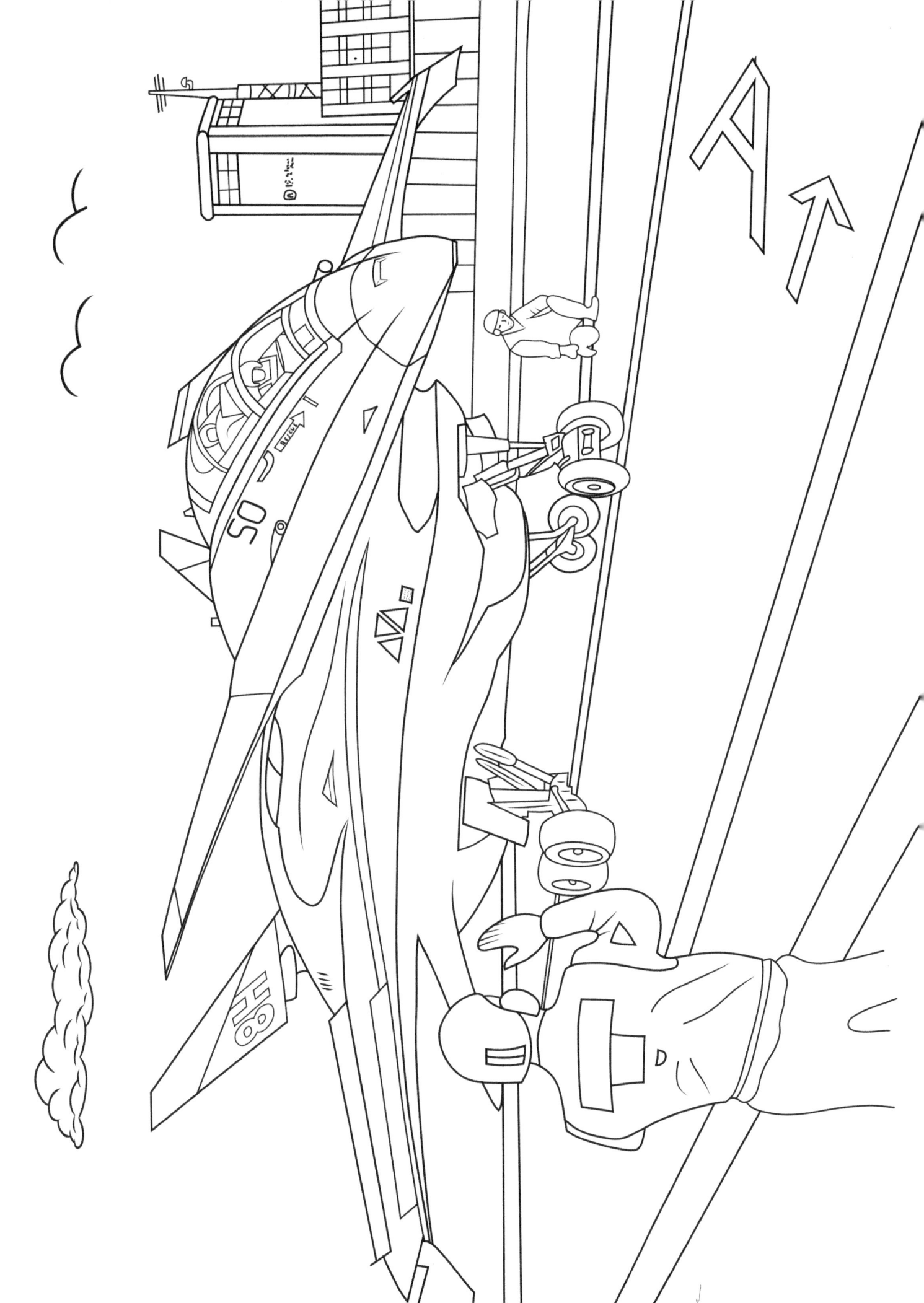

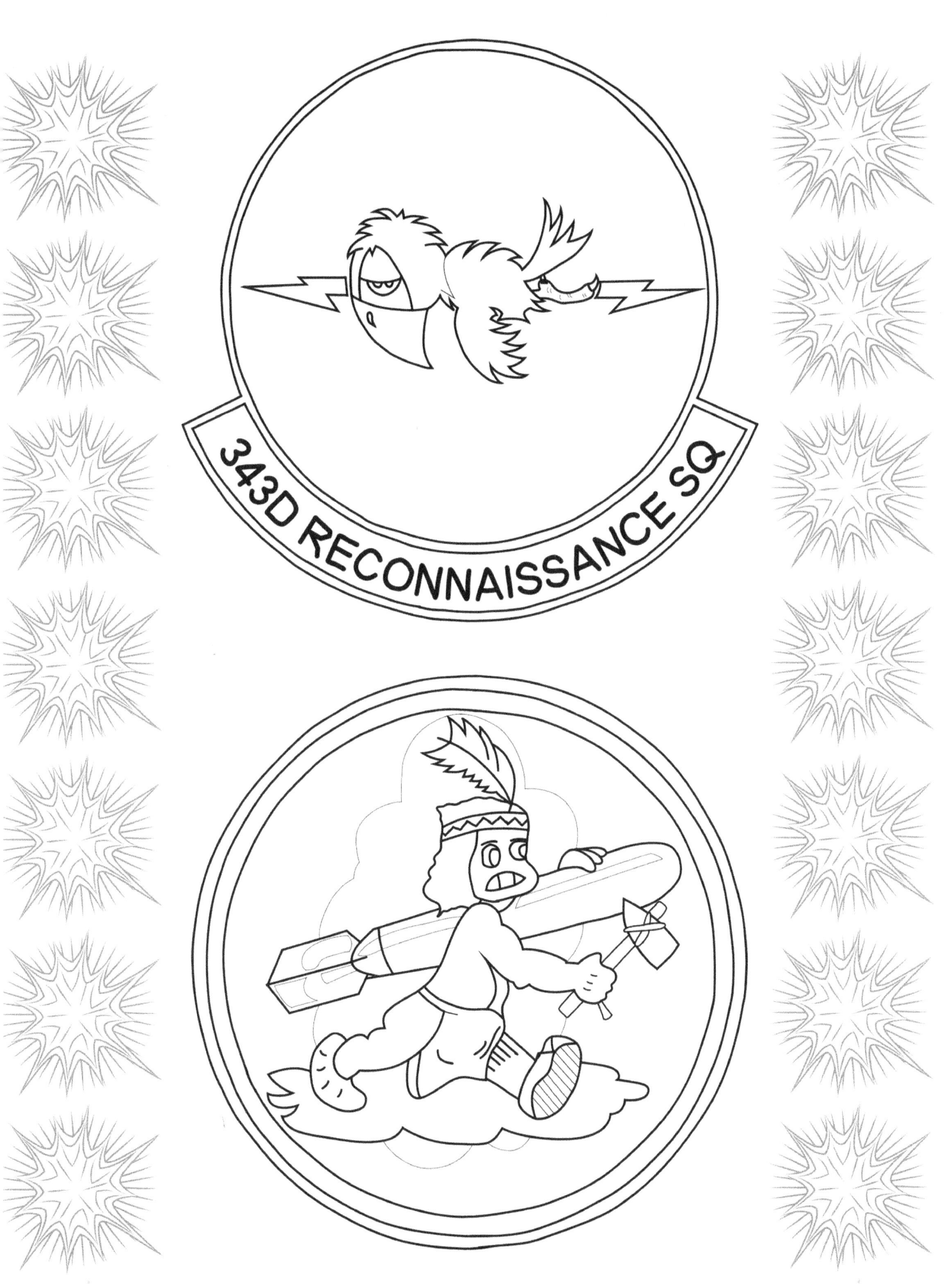

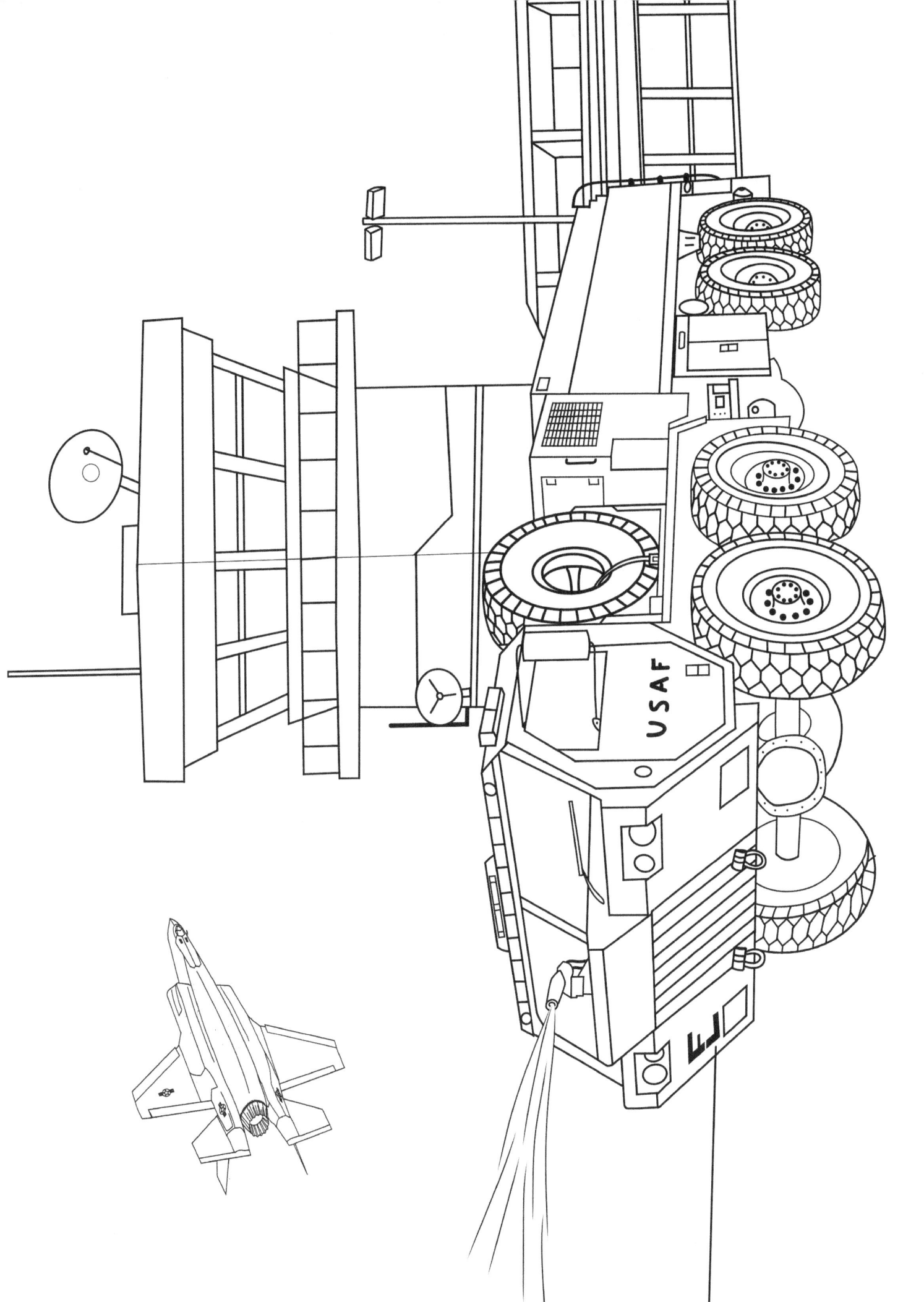

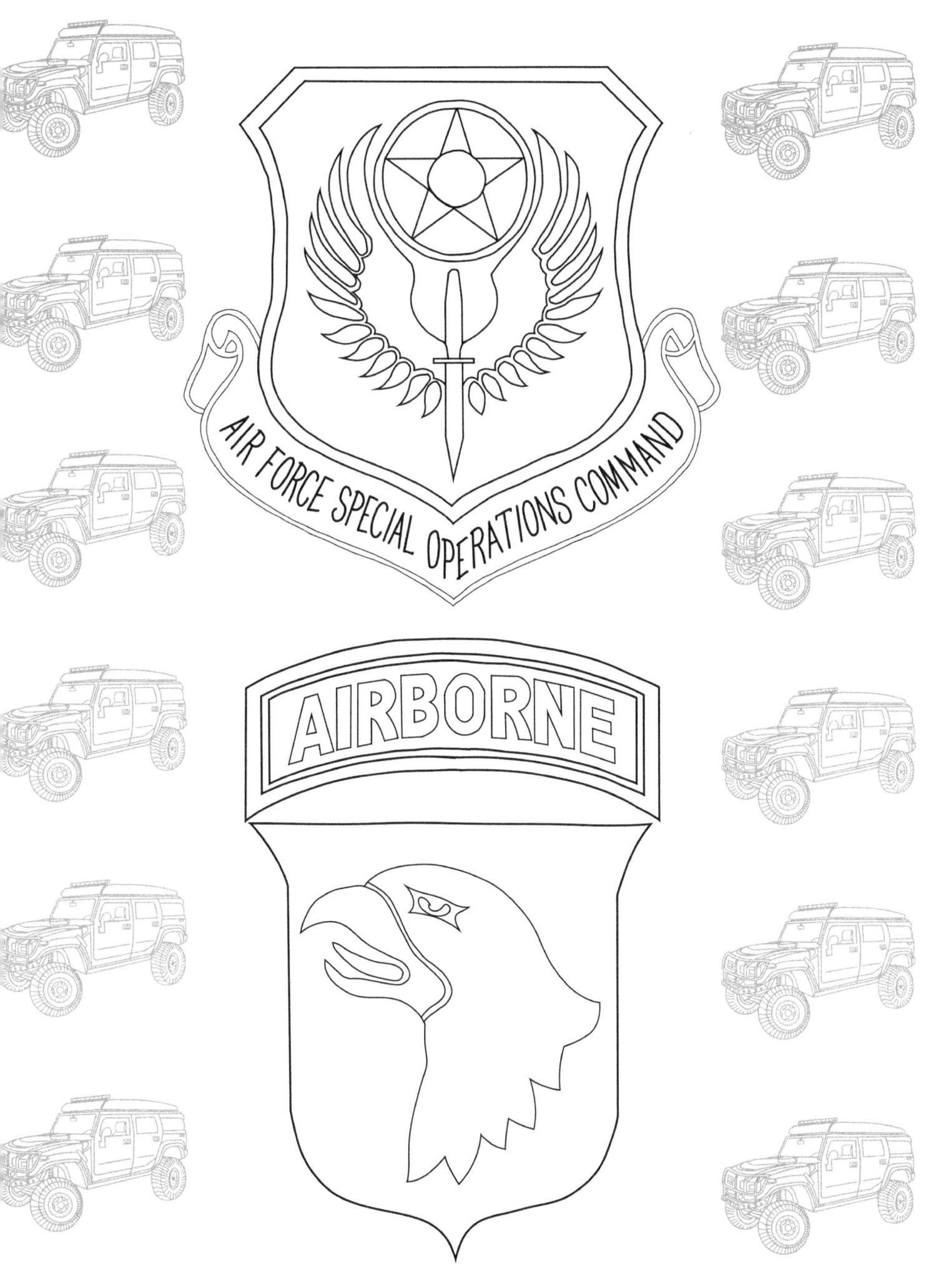

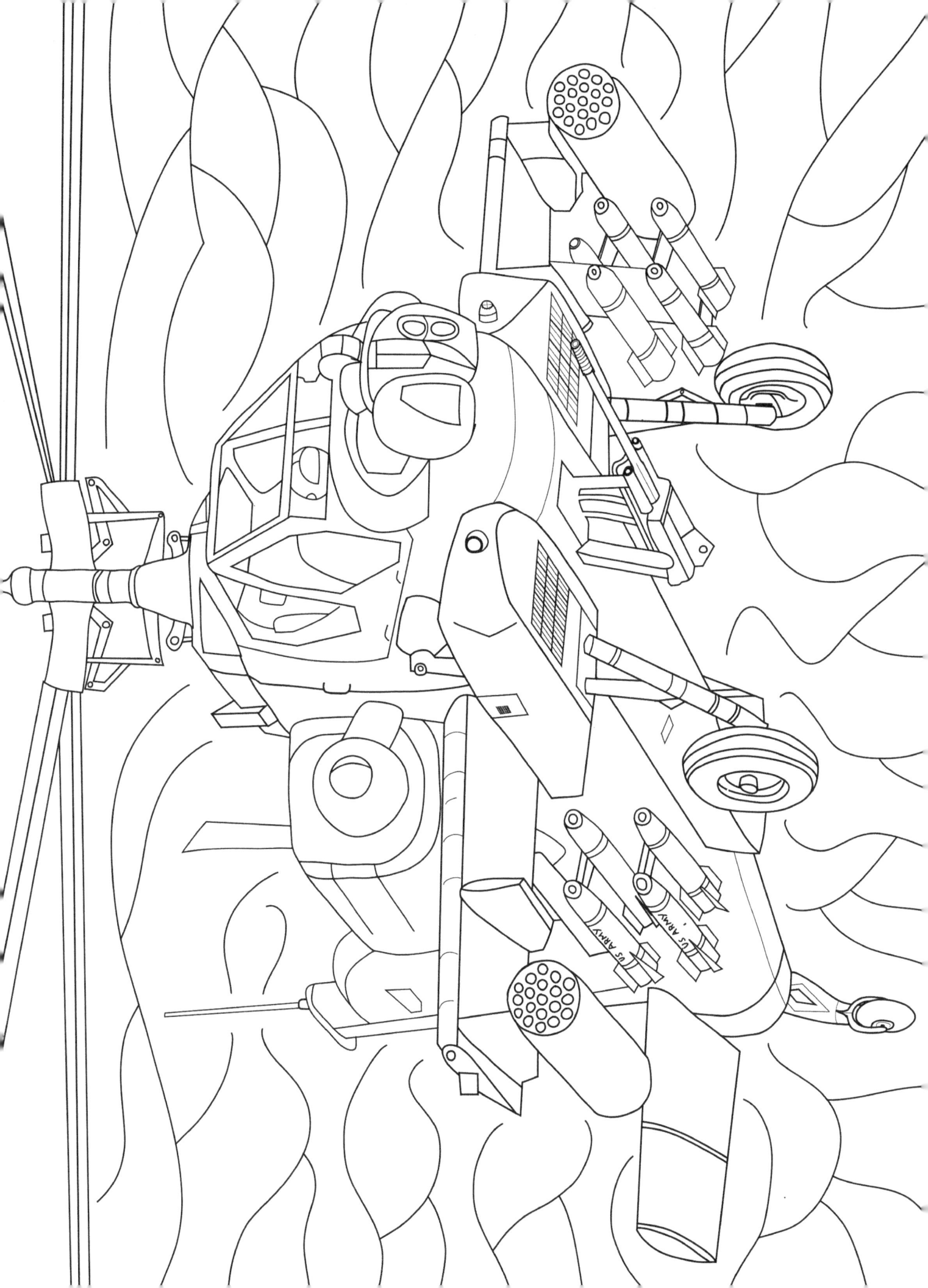

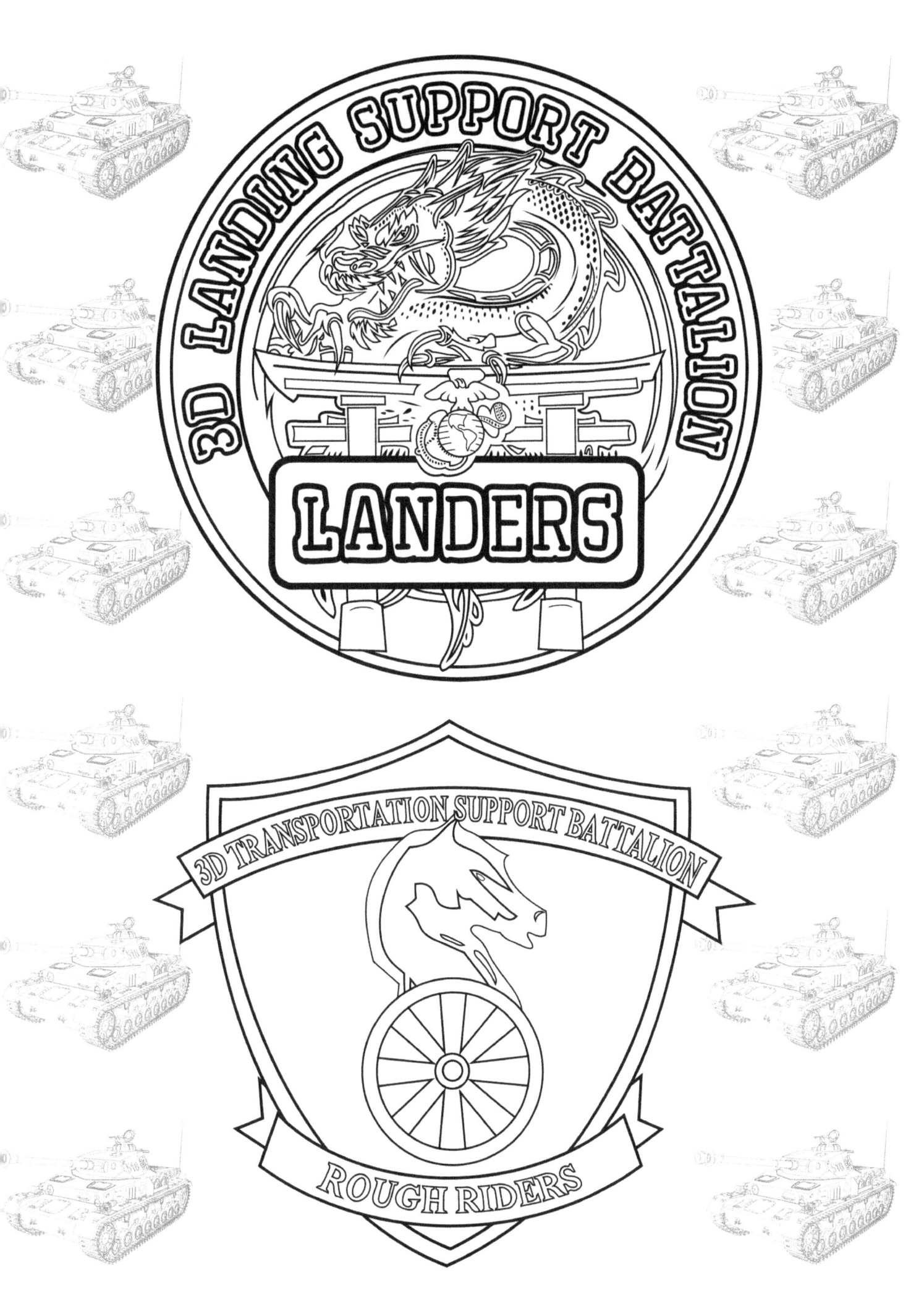

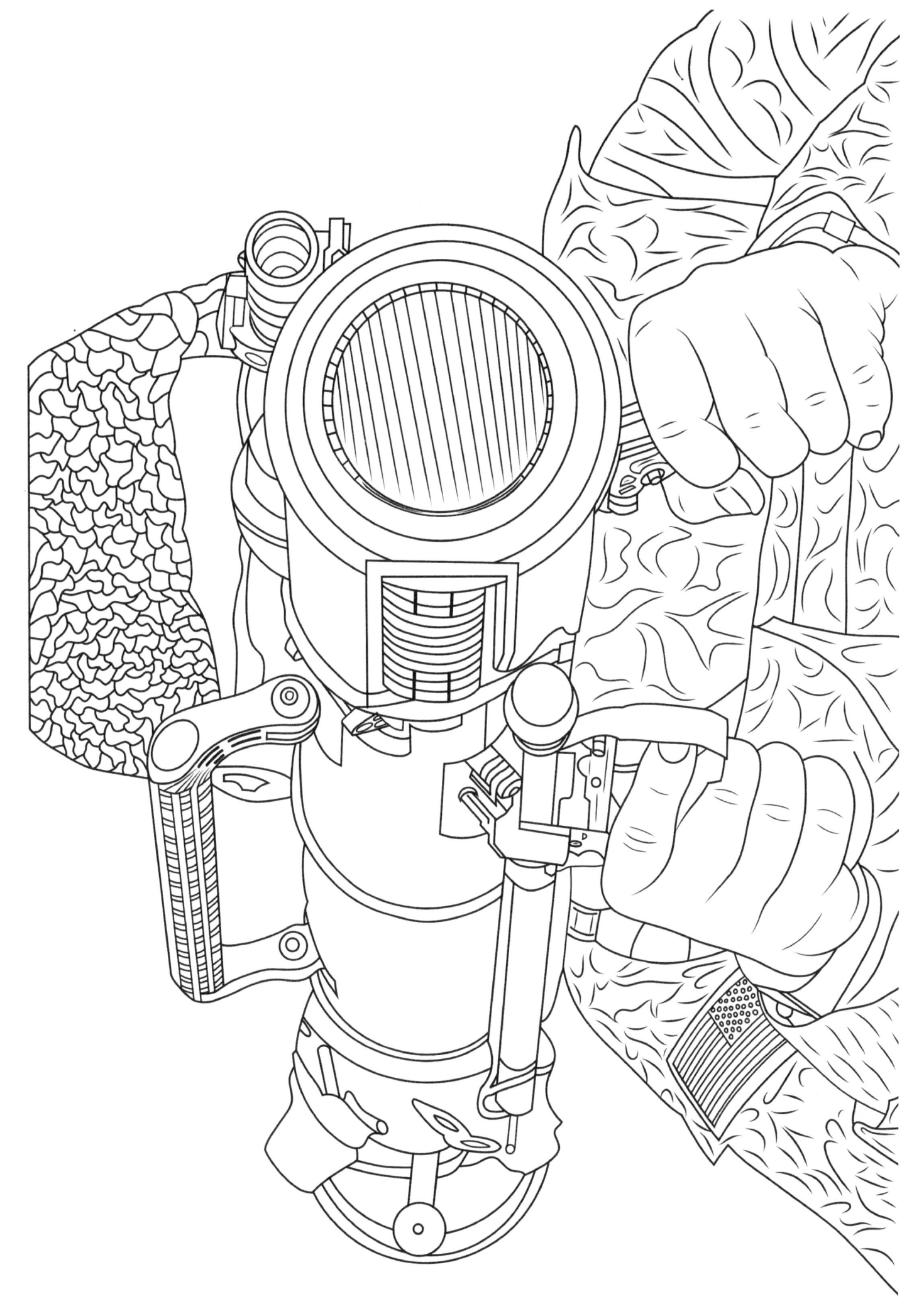

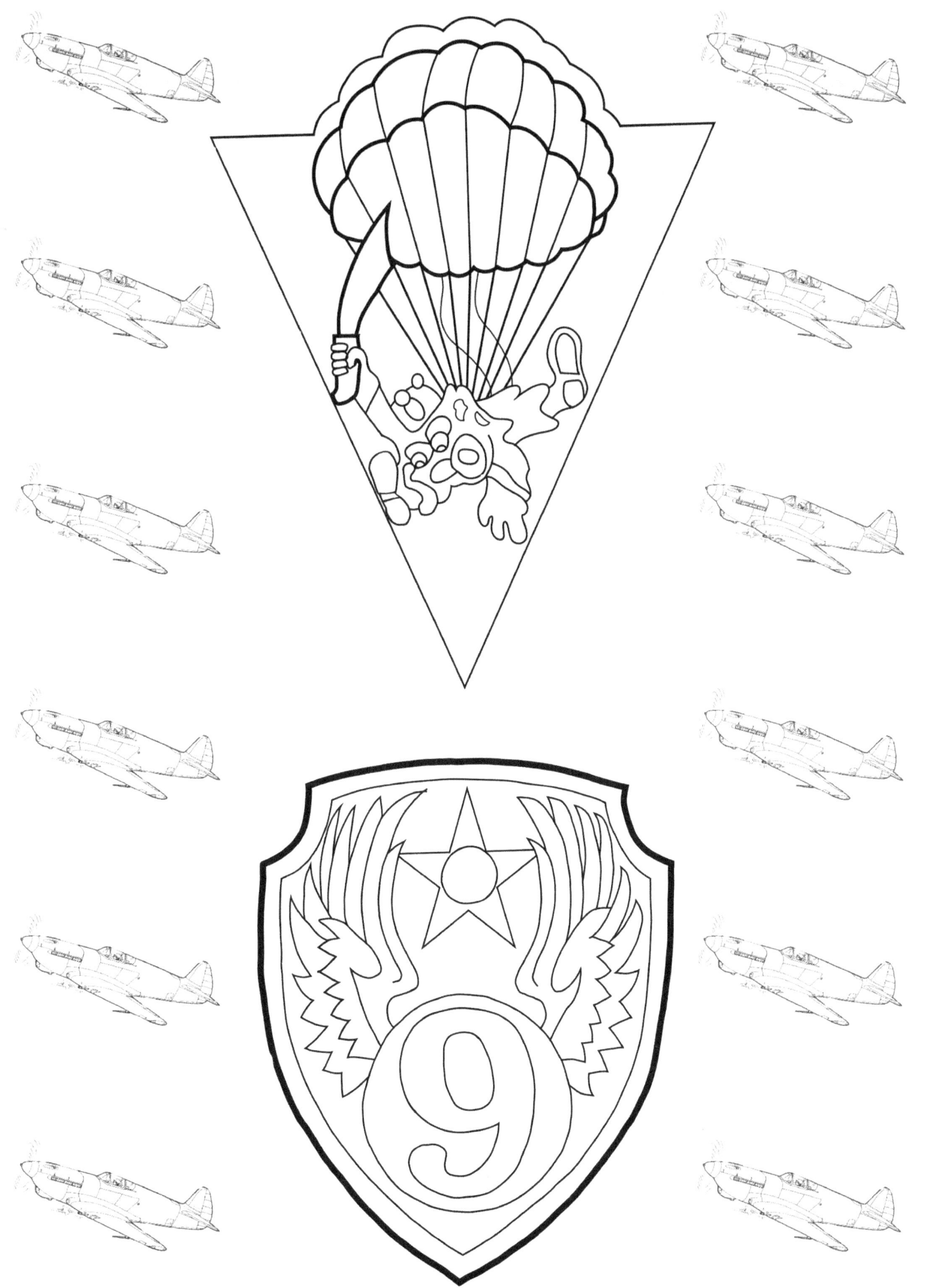

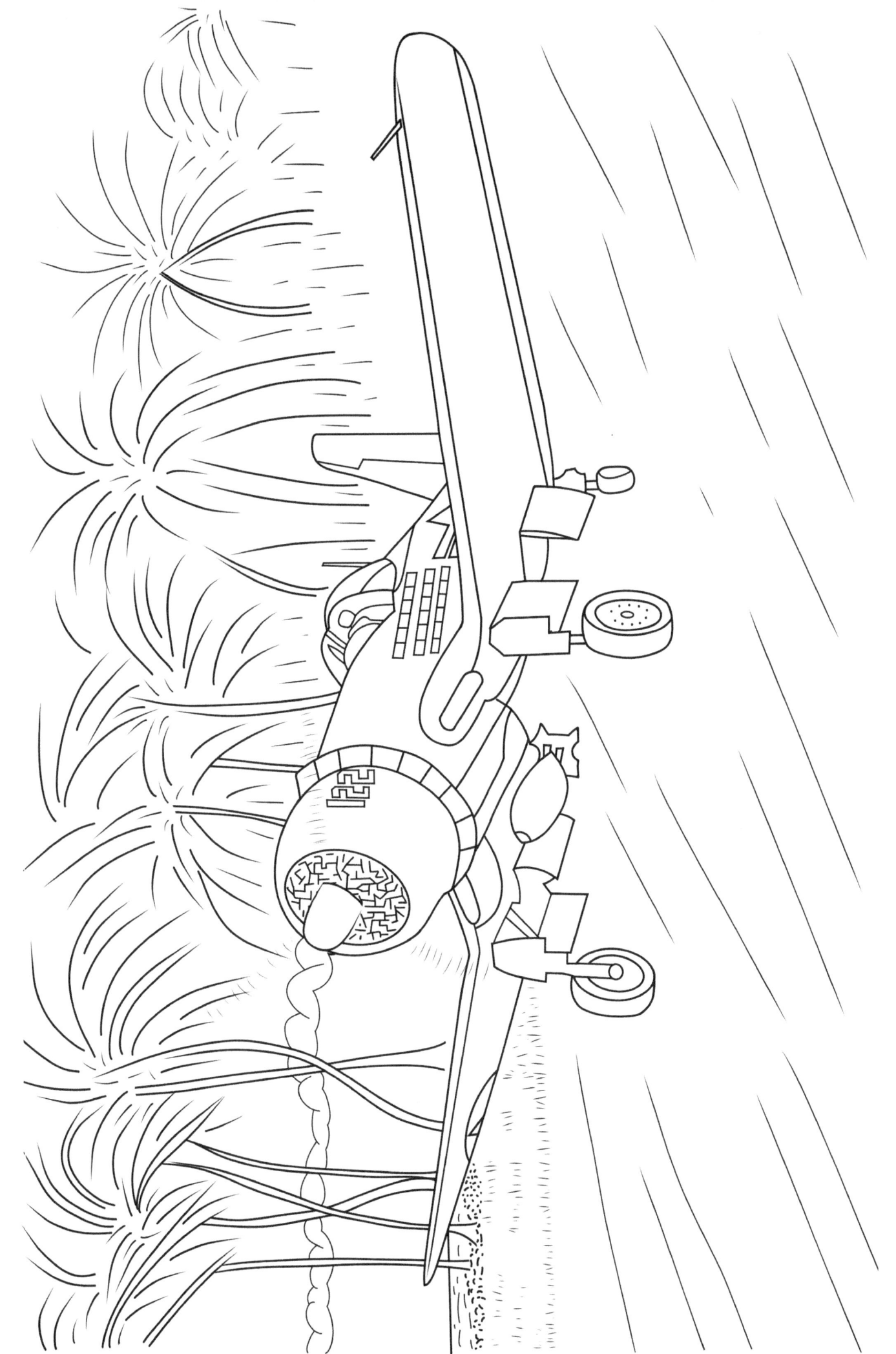

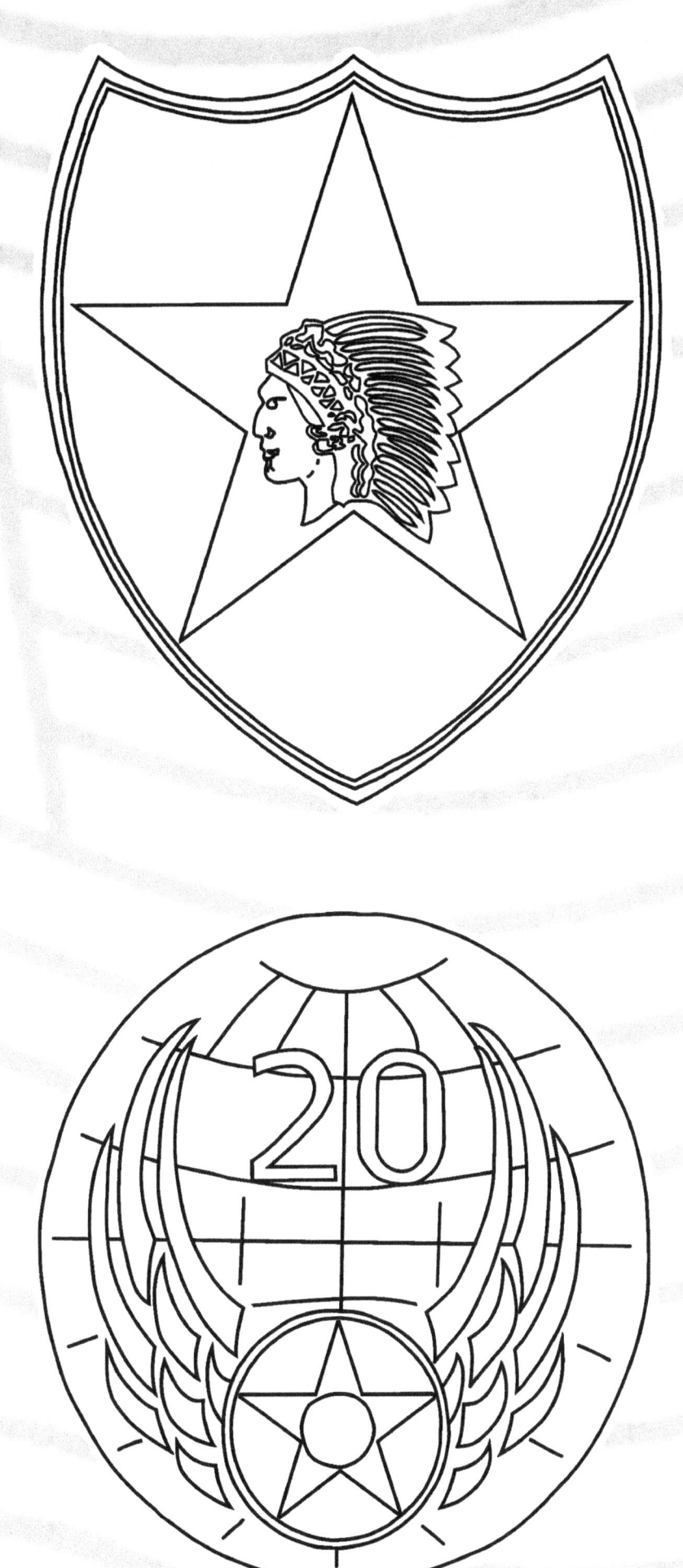

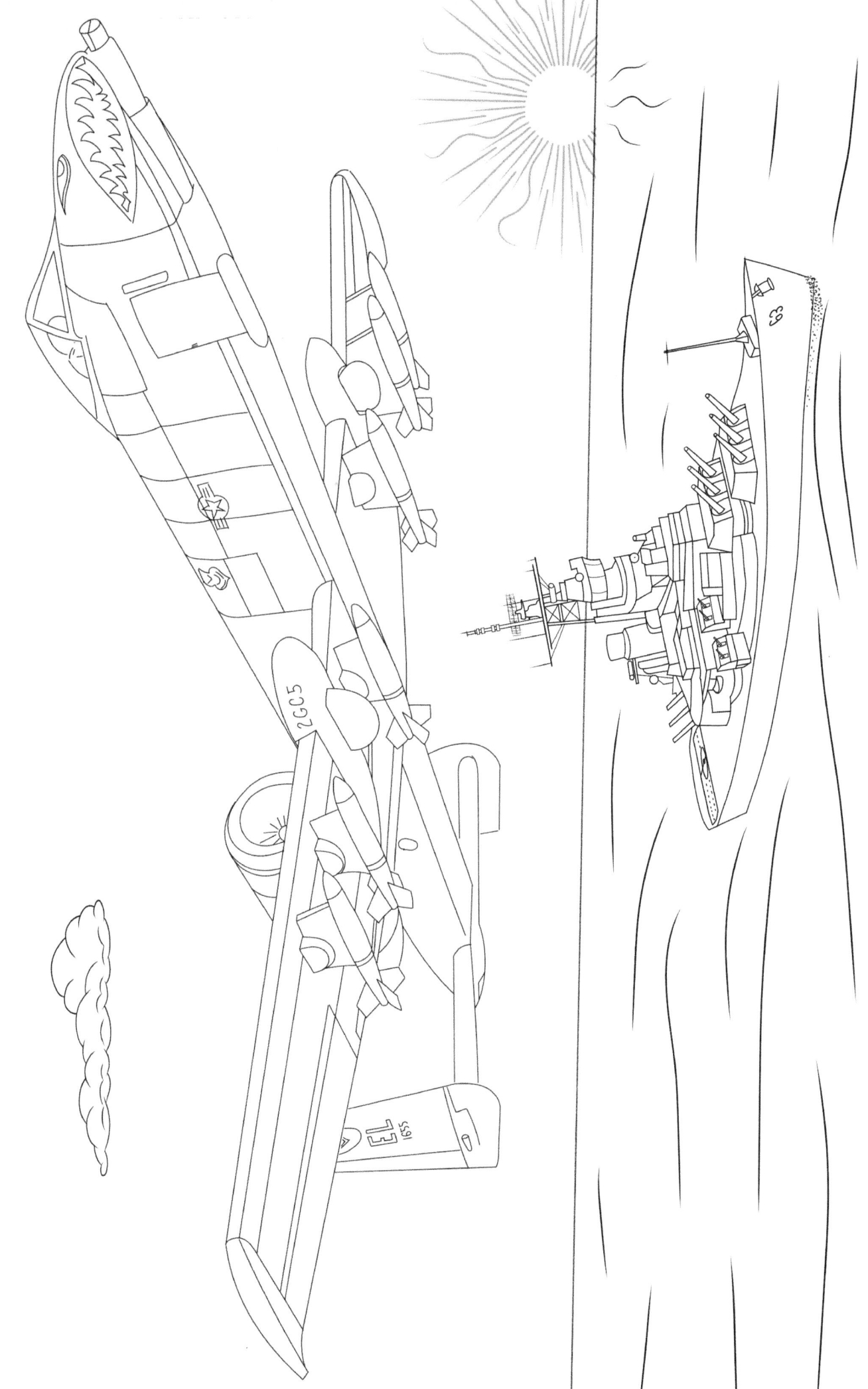

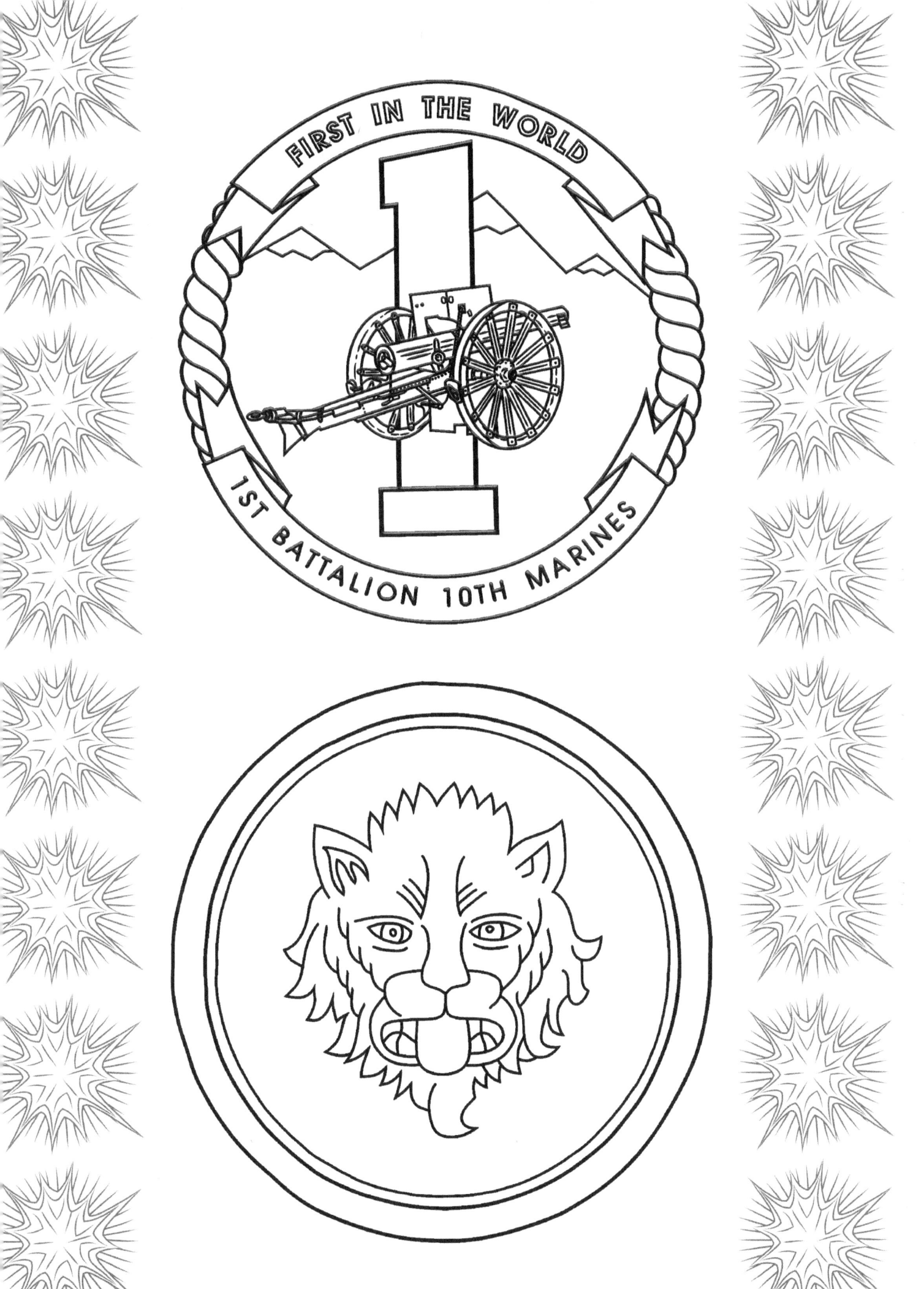

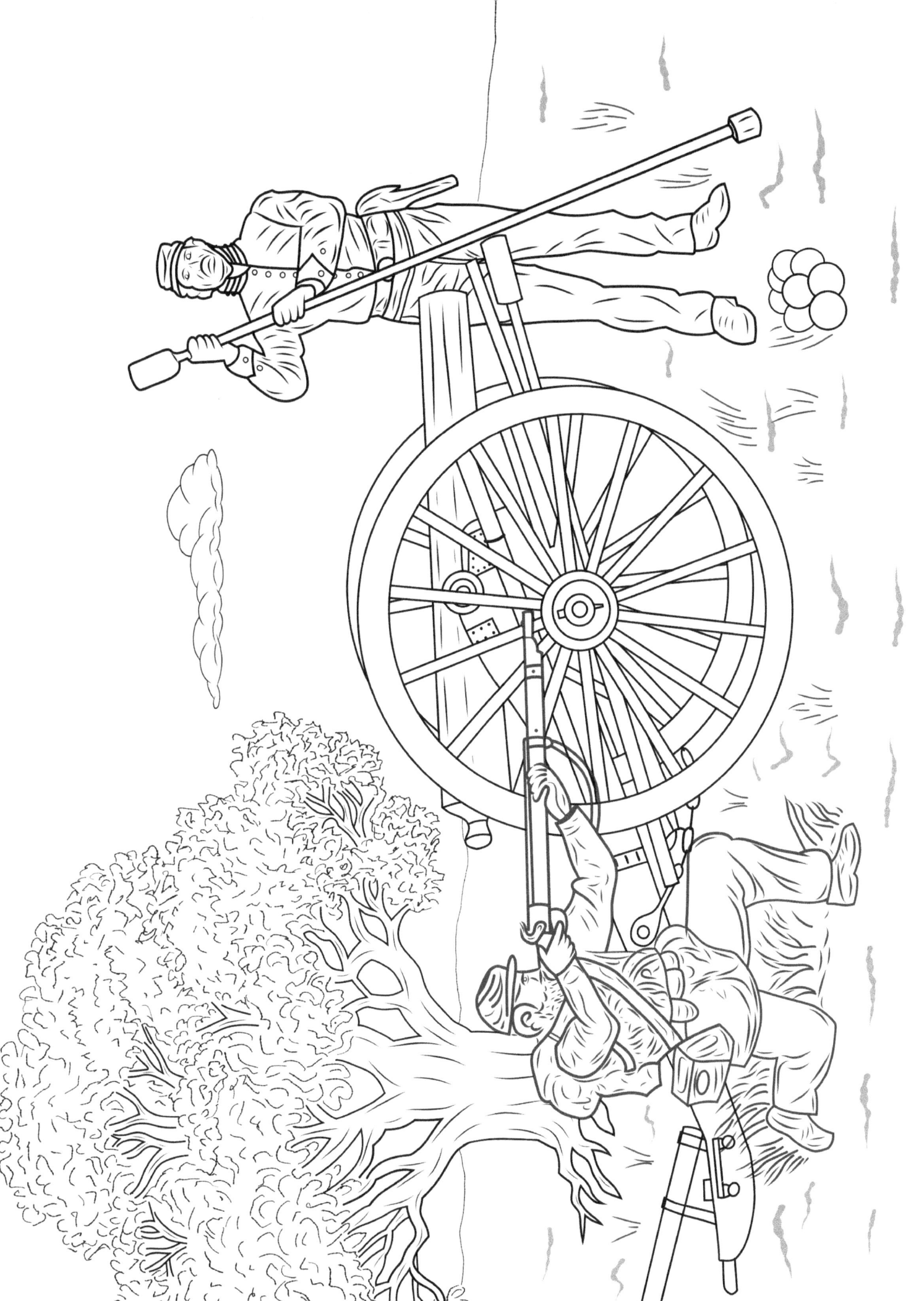

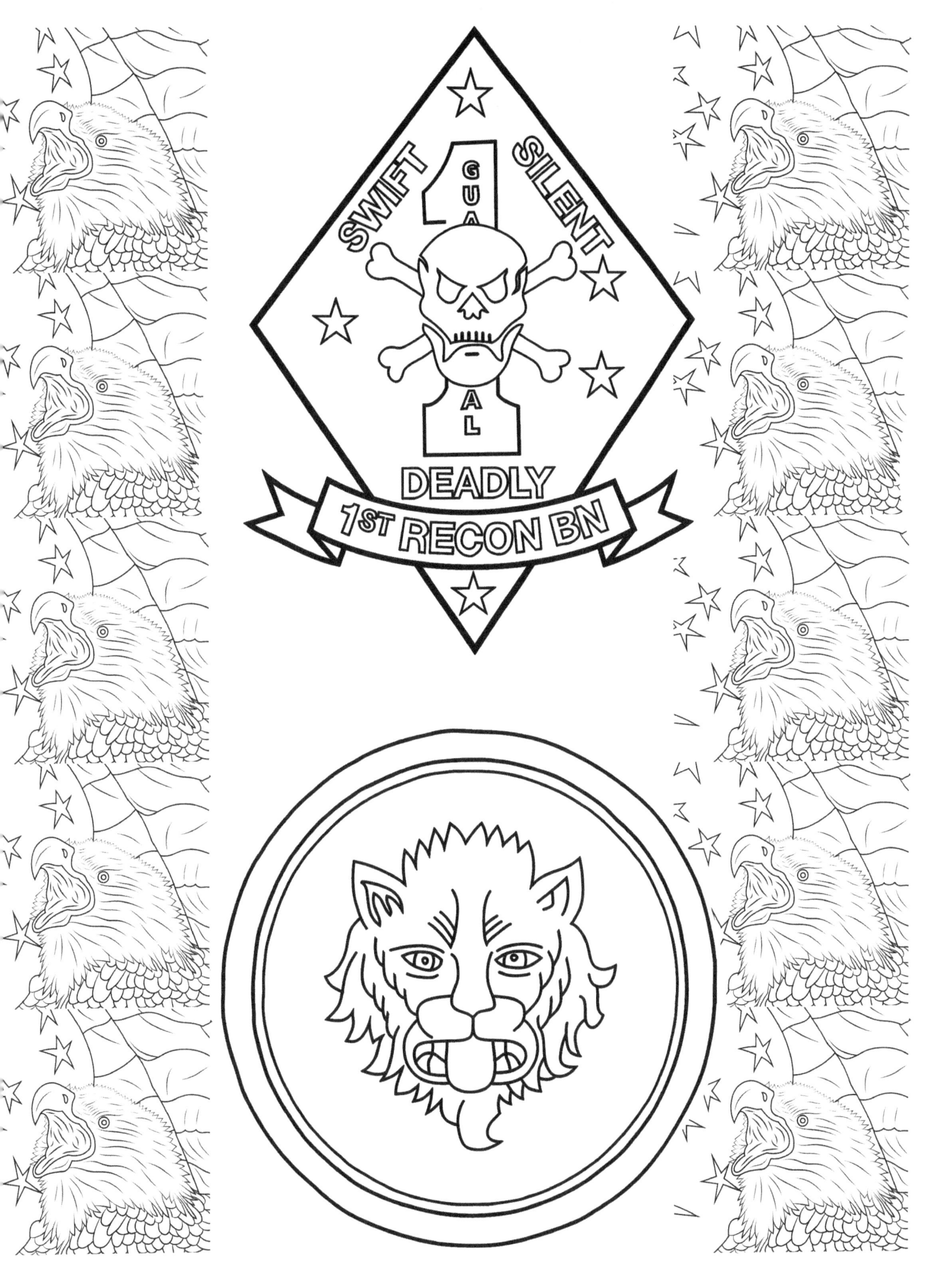

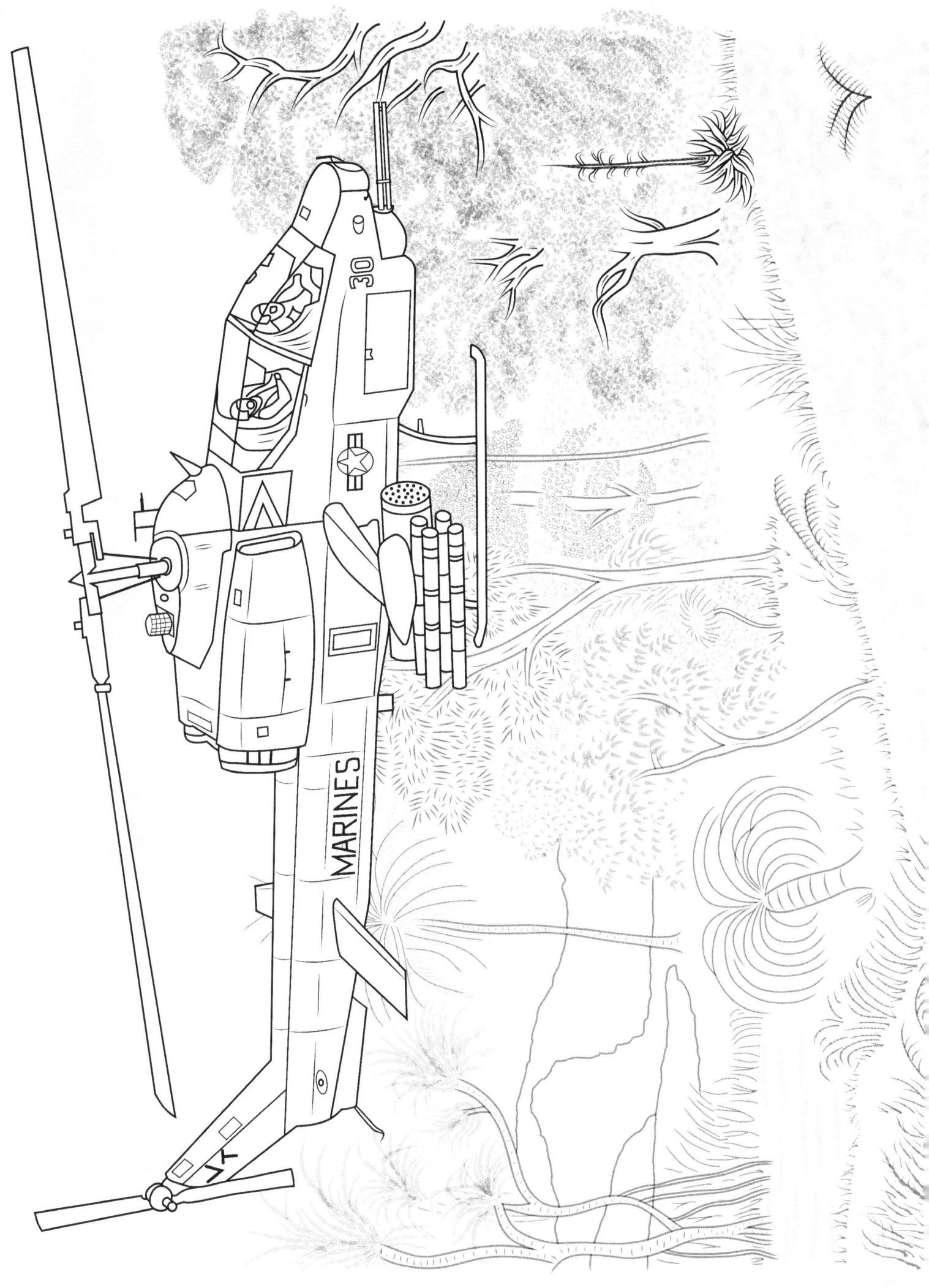

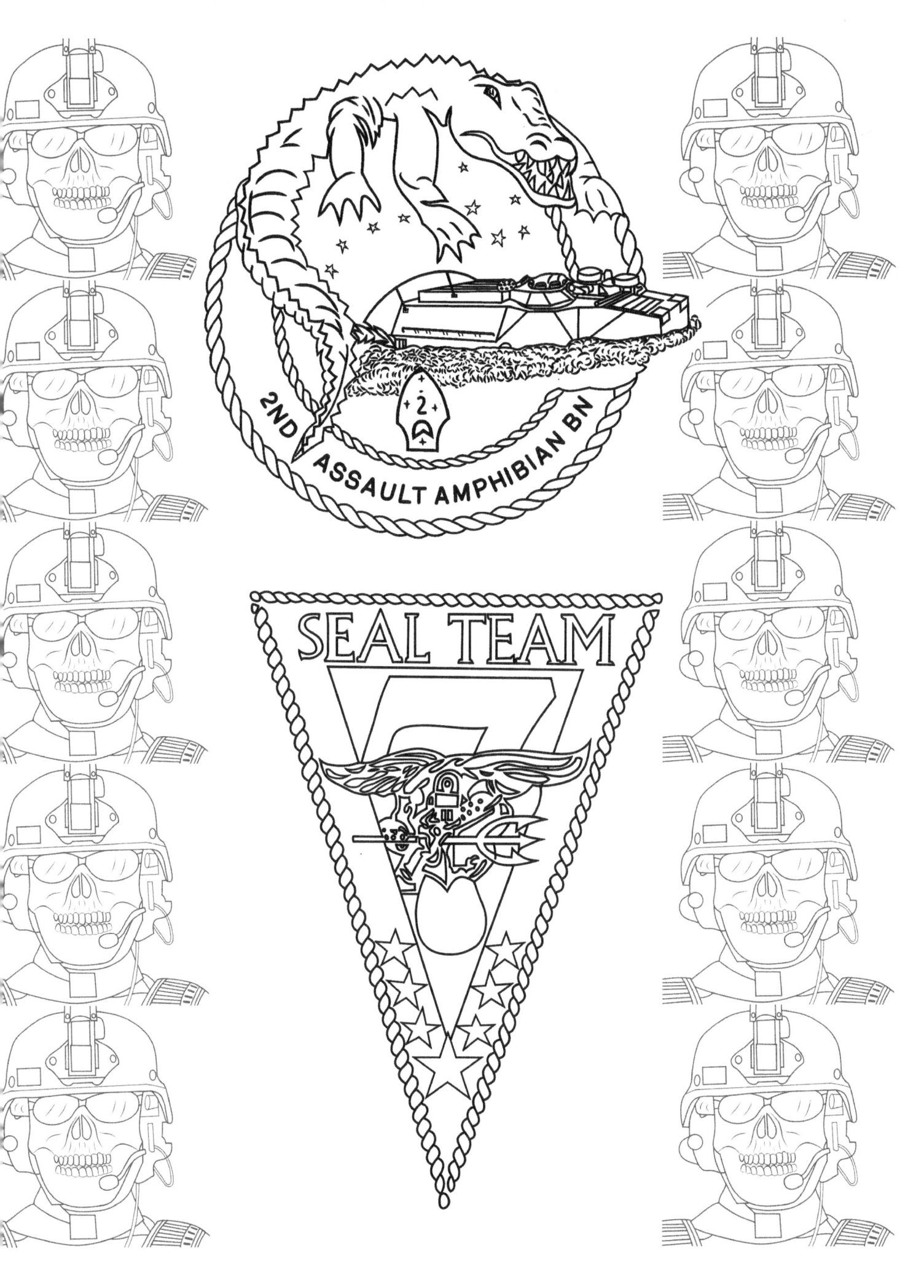

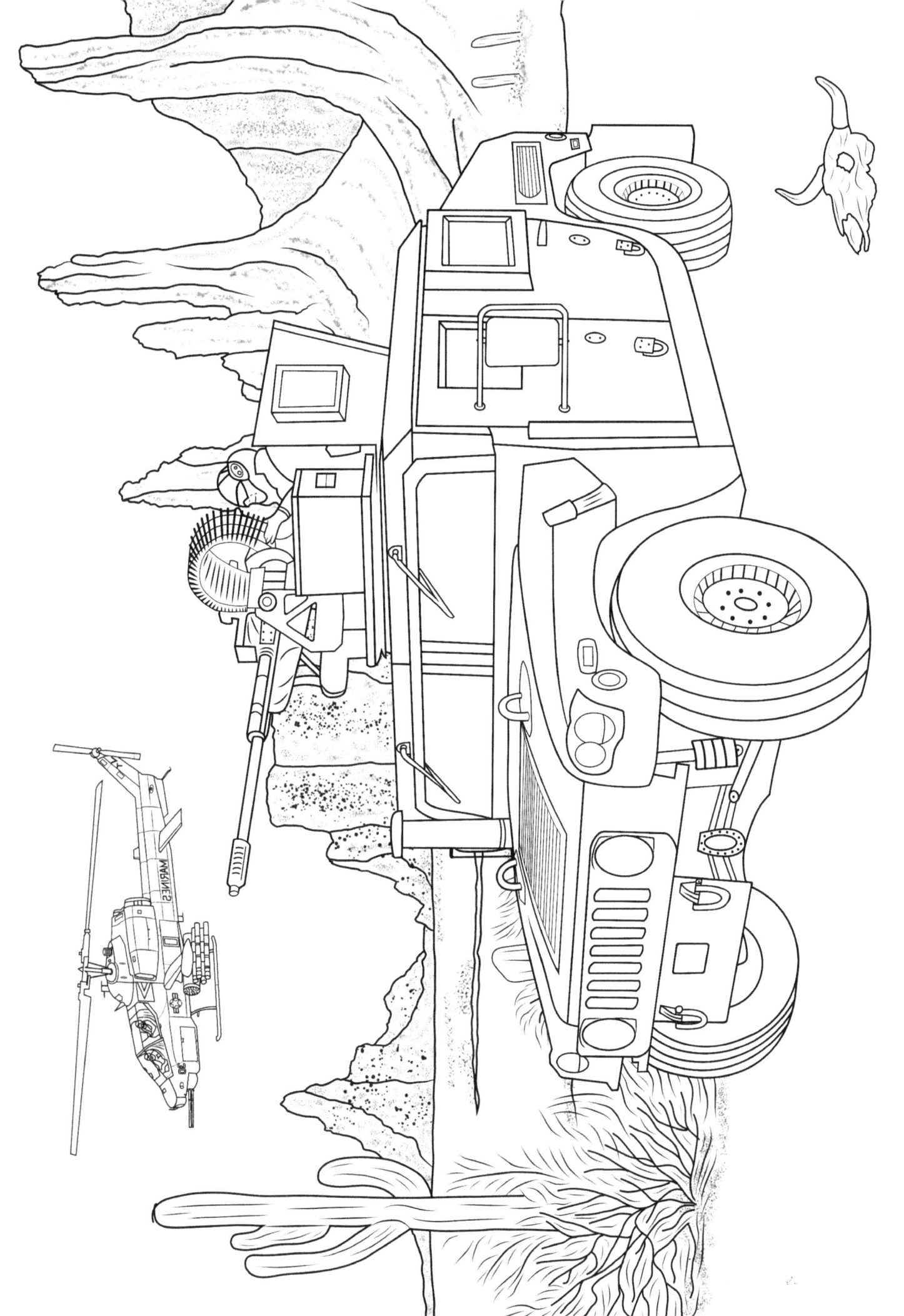

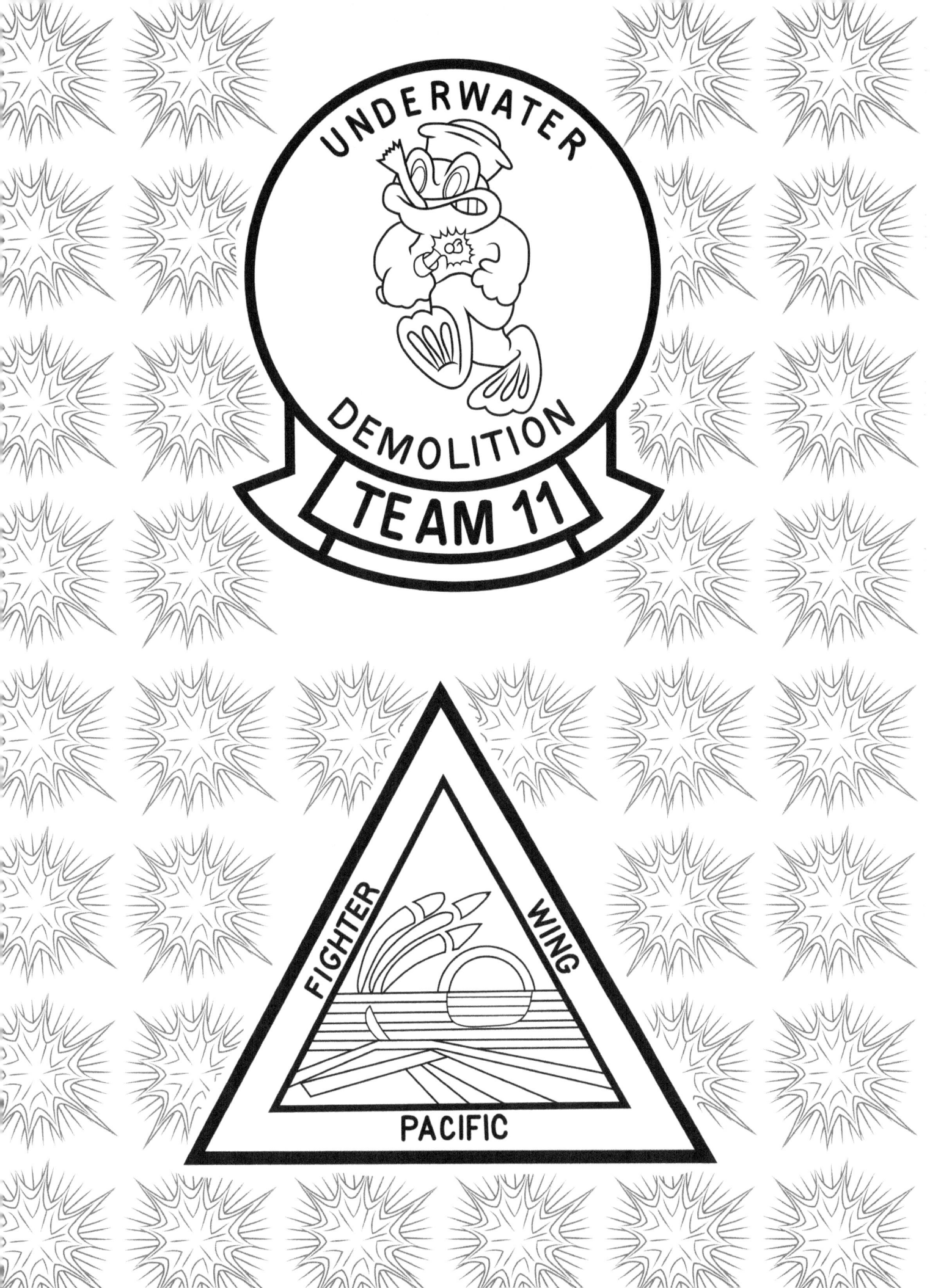

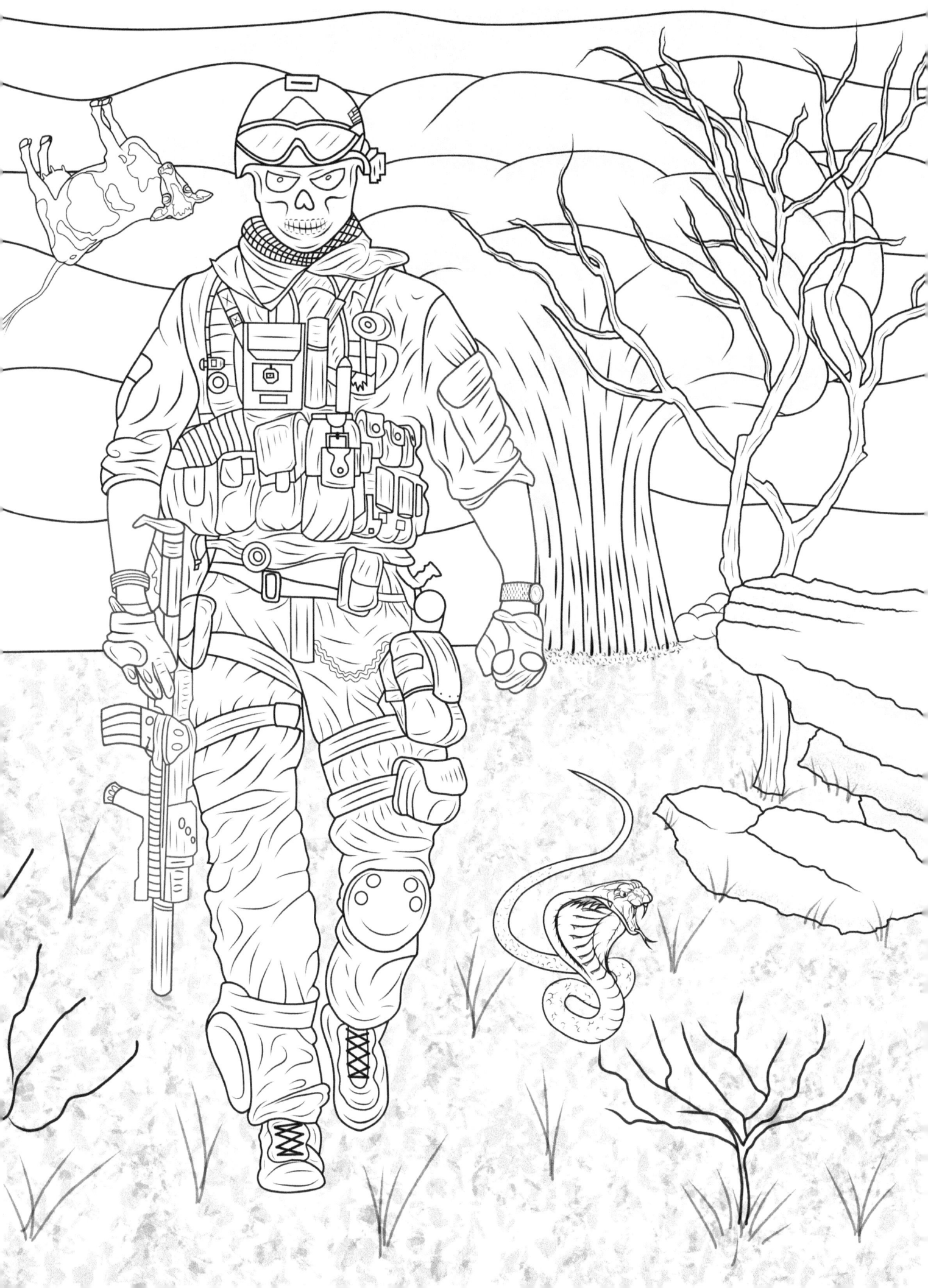

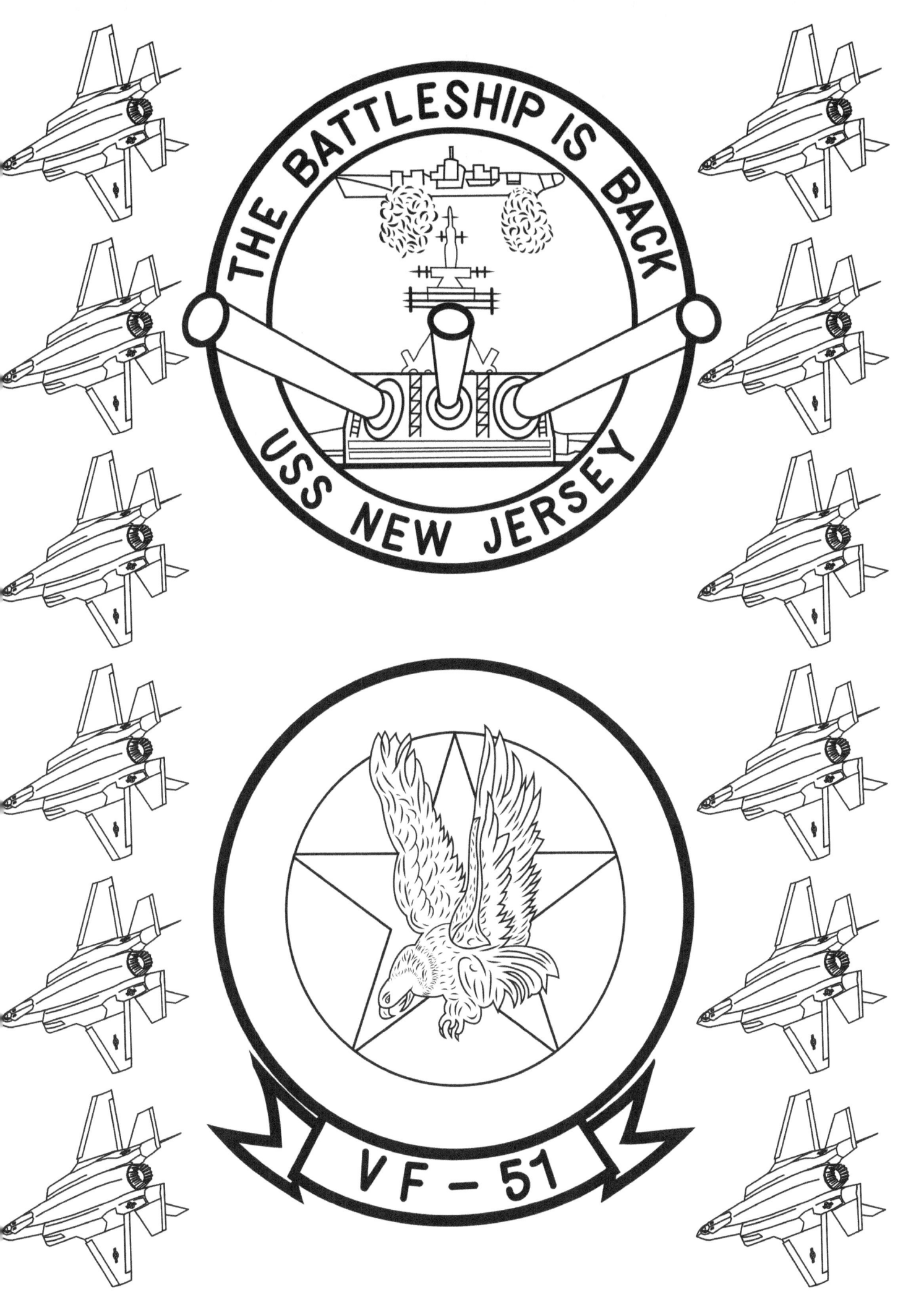

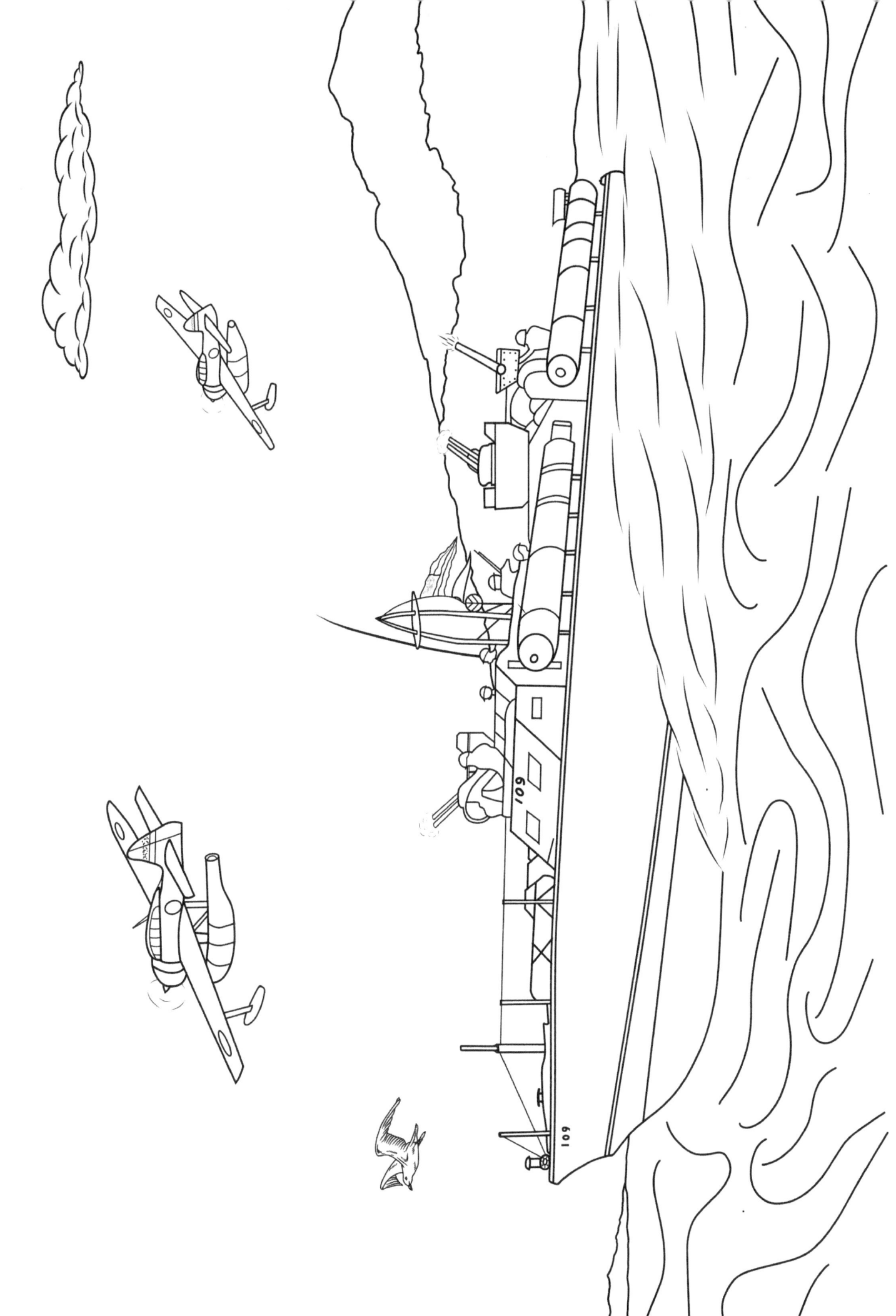

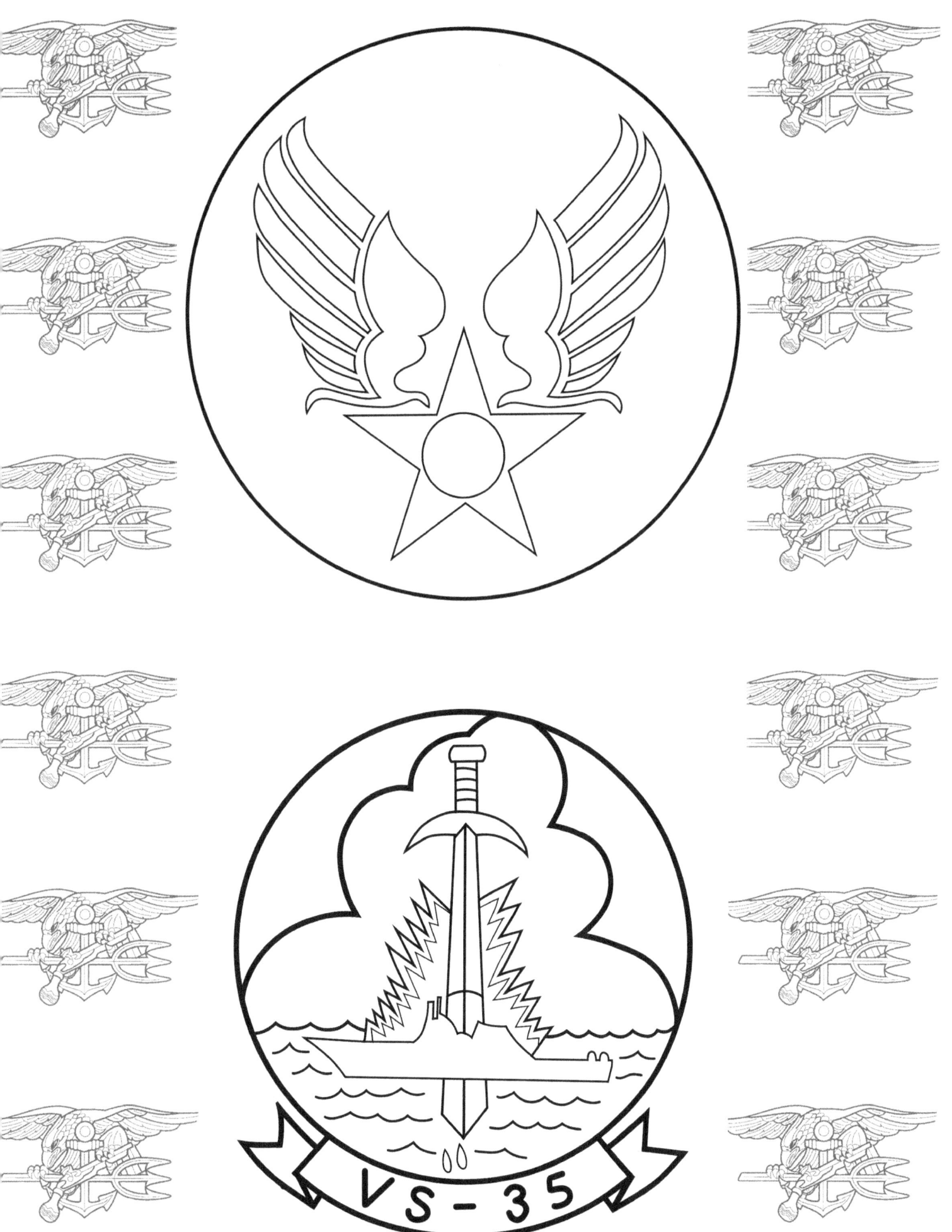

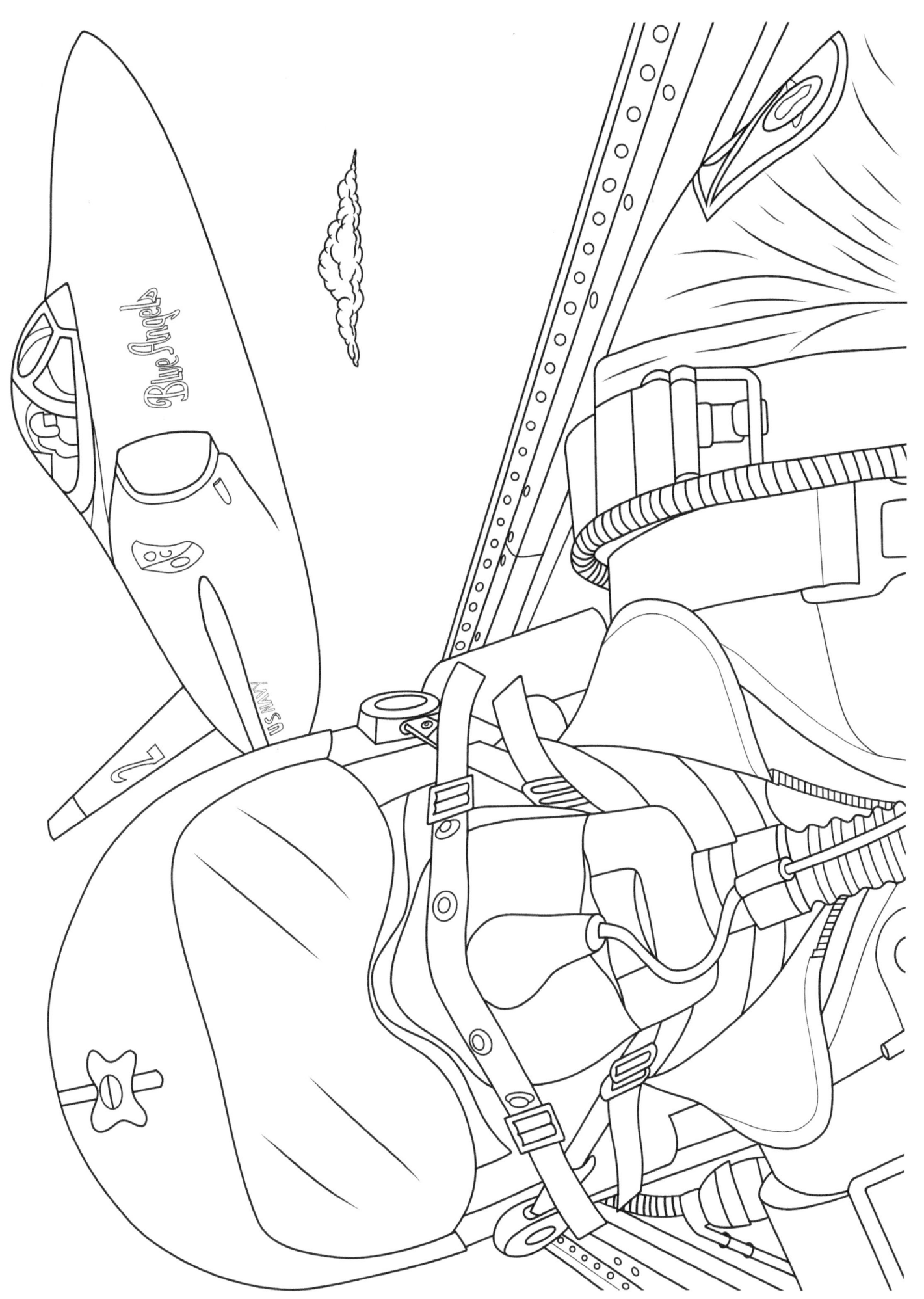

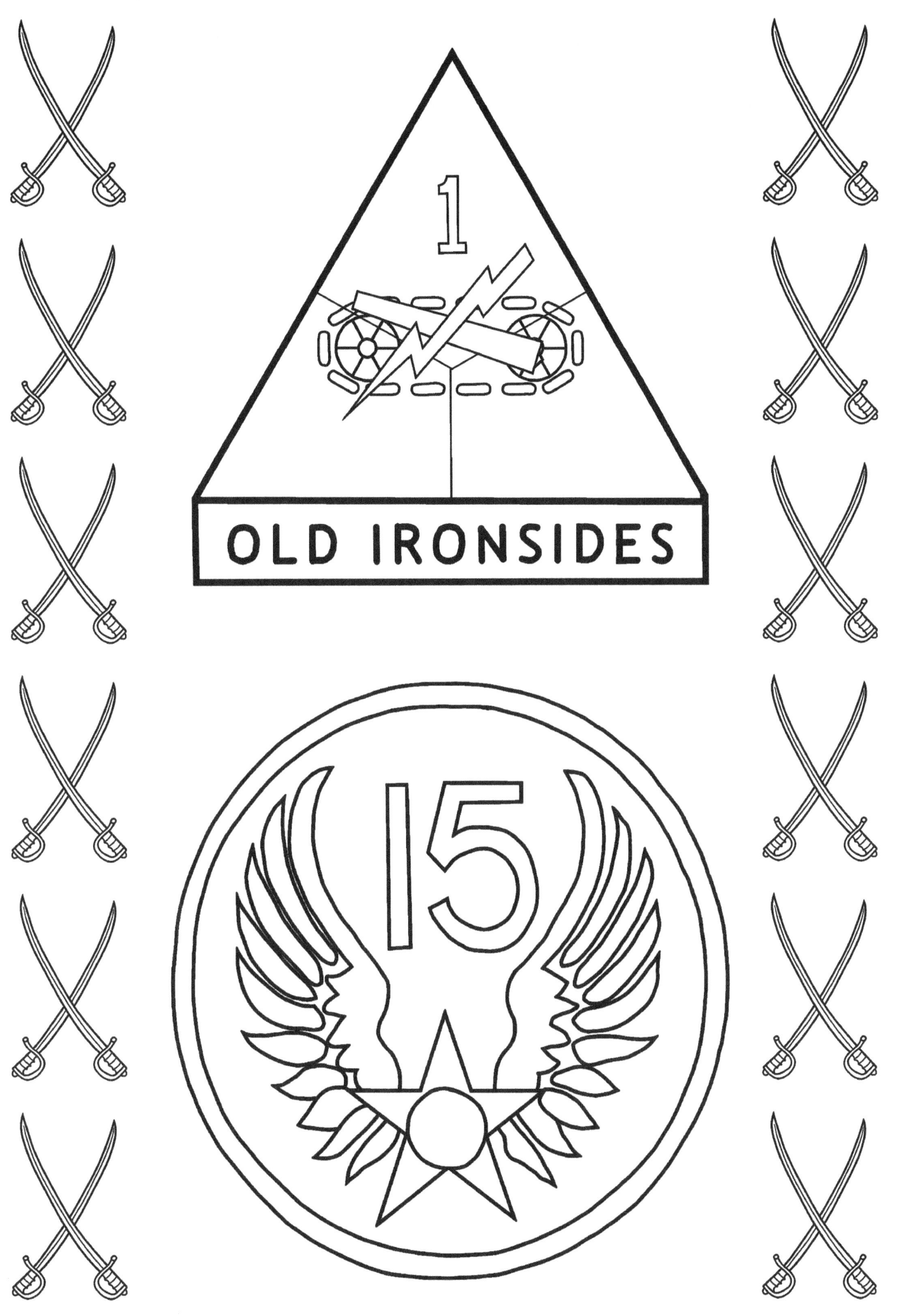

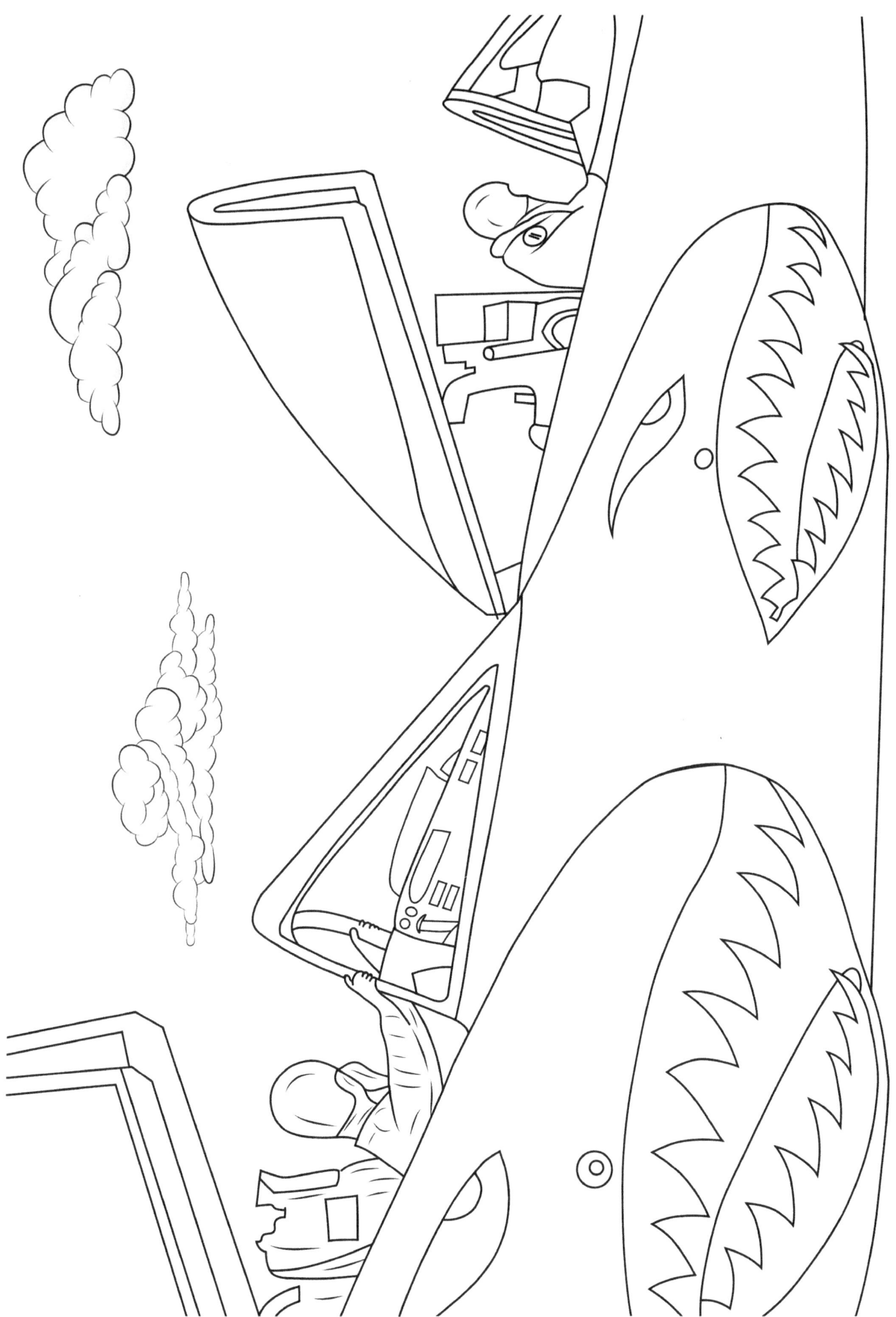

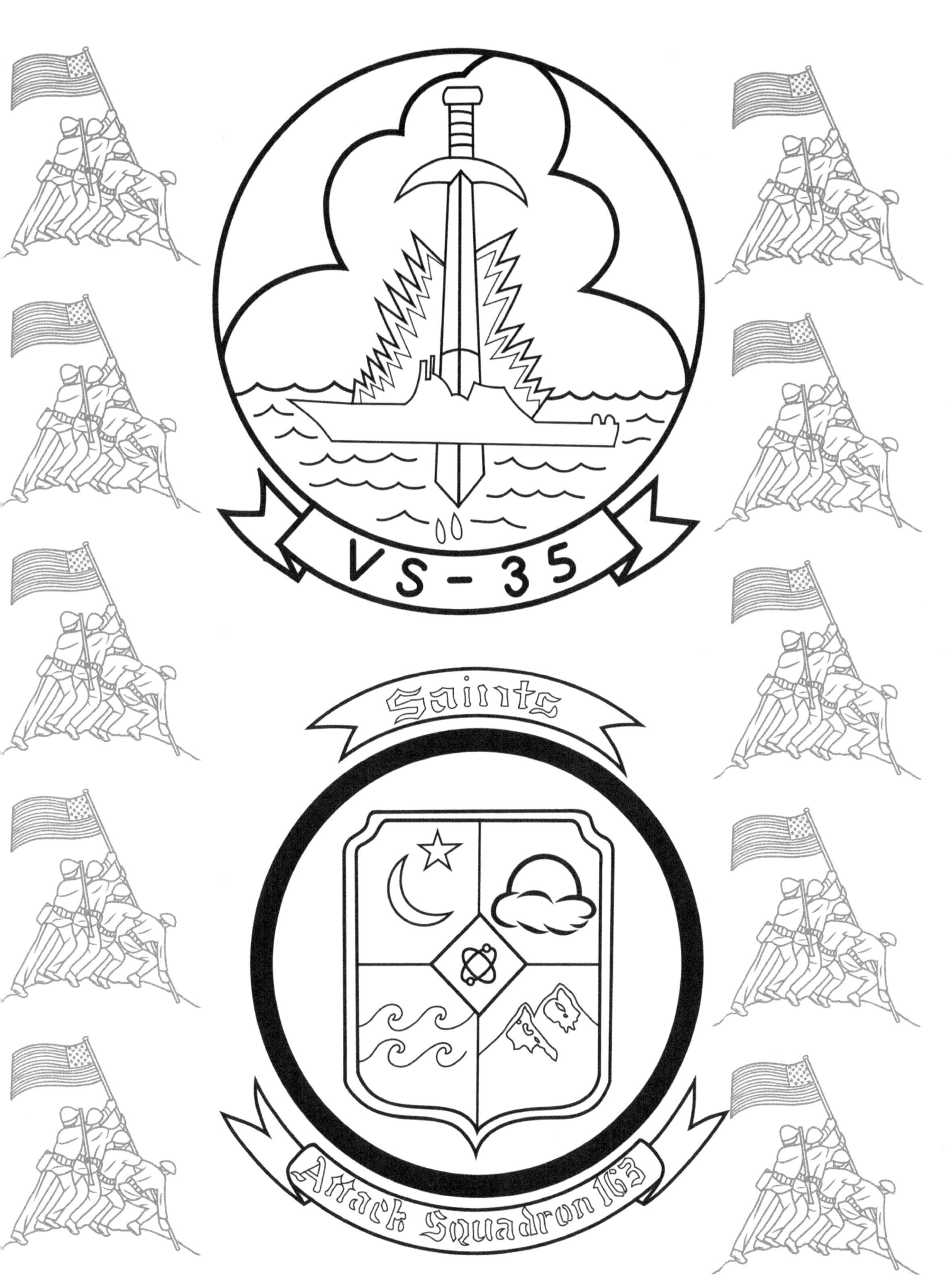

VS - 35

Saints

Attack Squadron 163

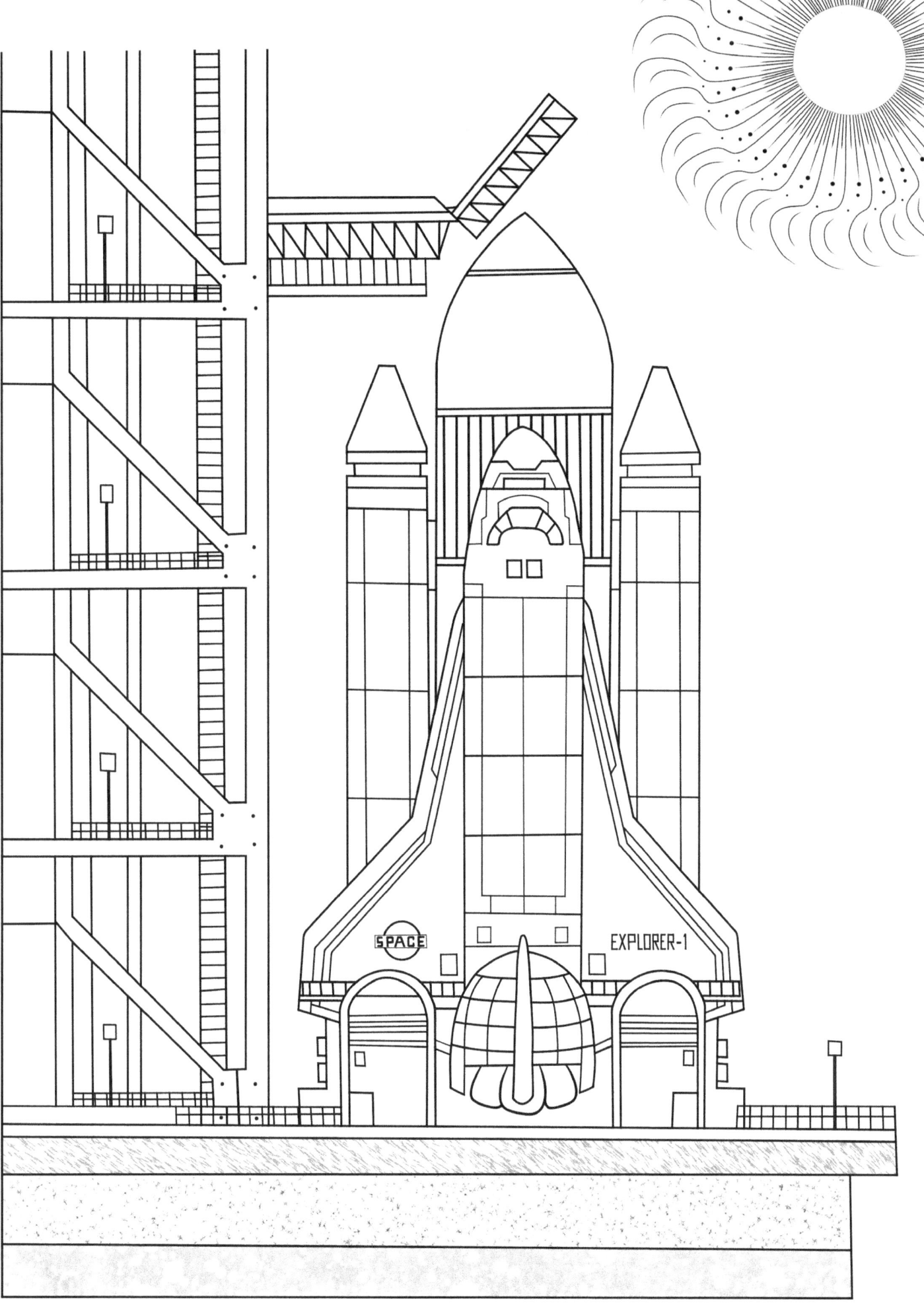

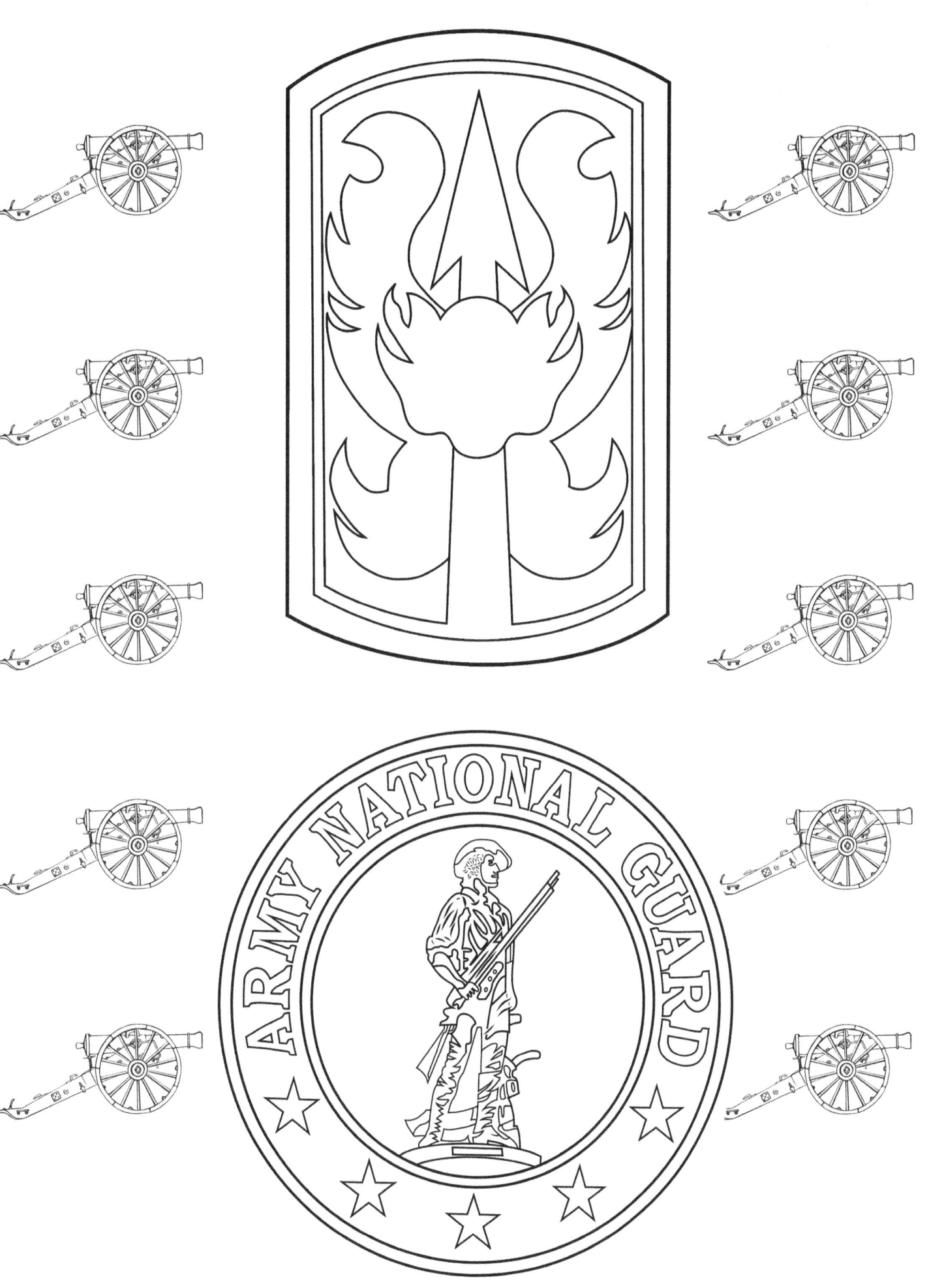

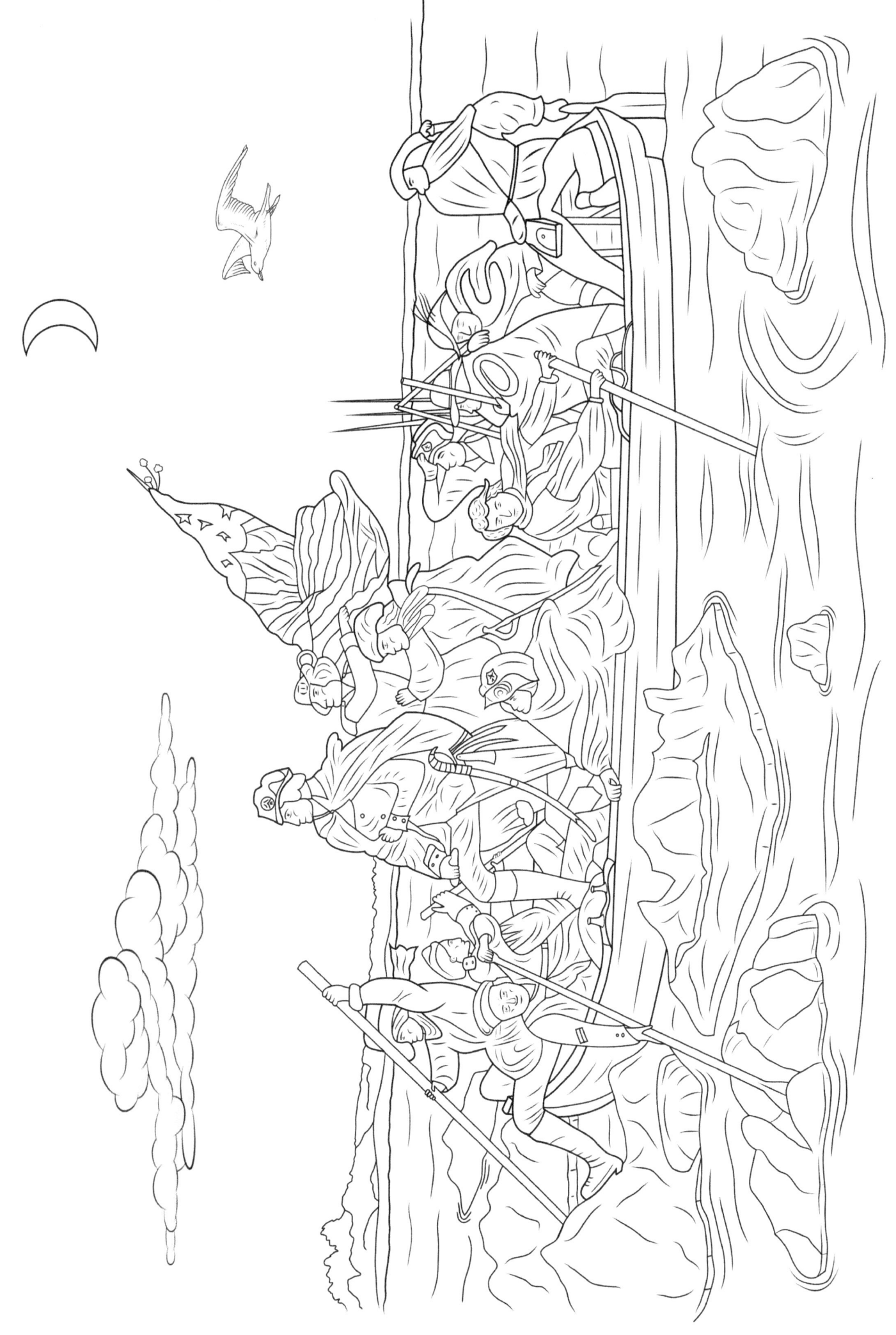

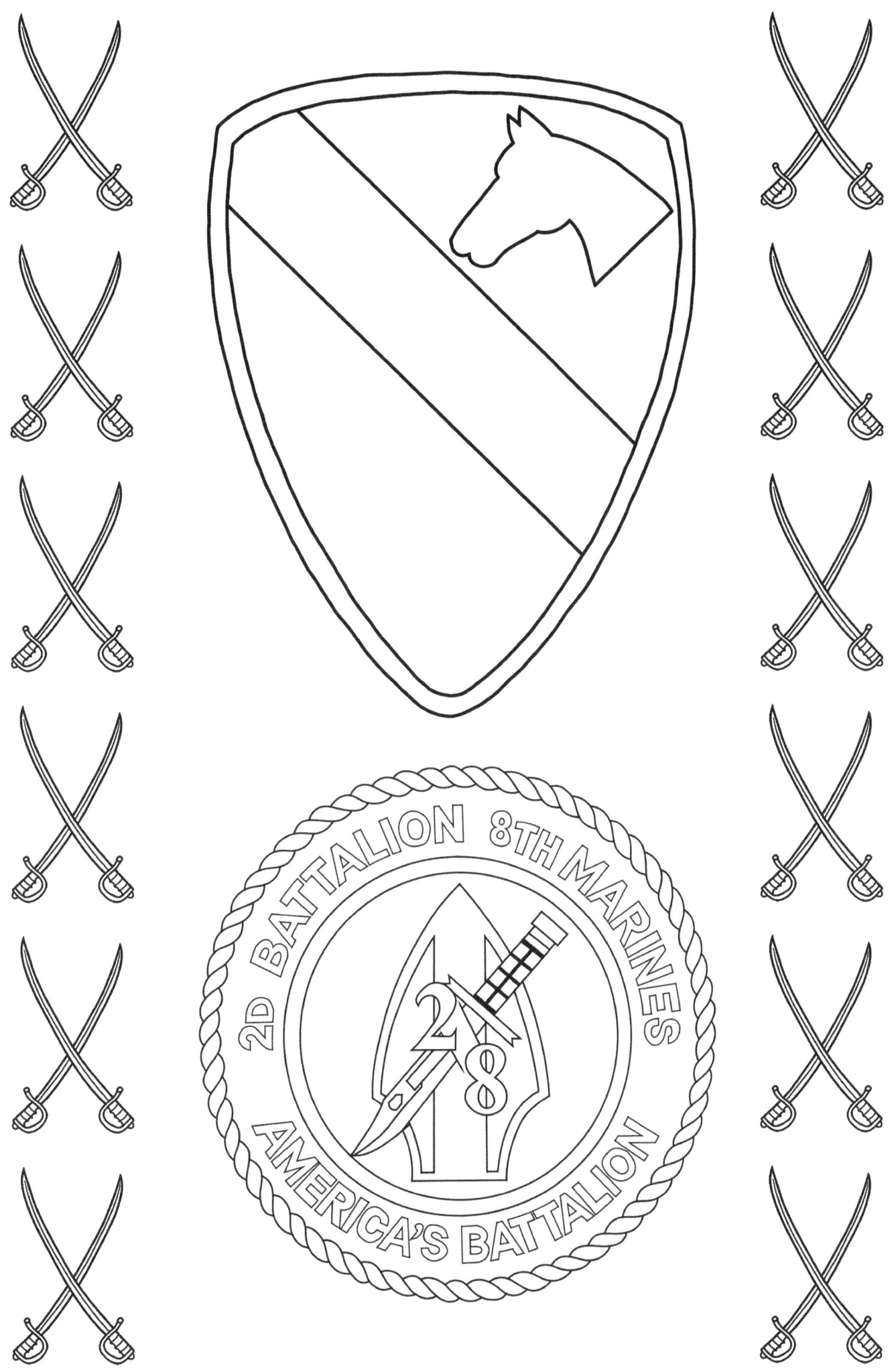

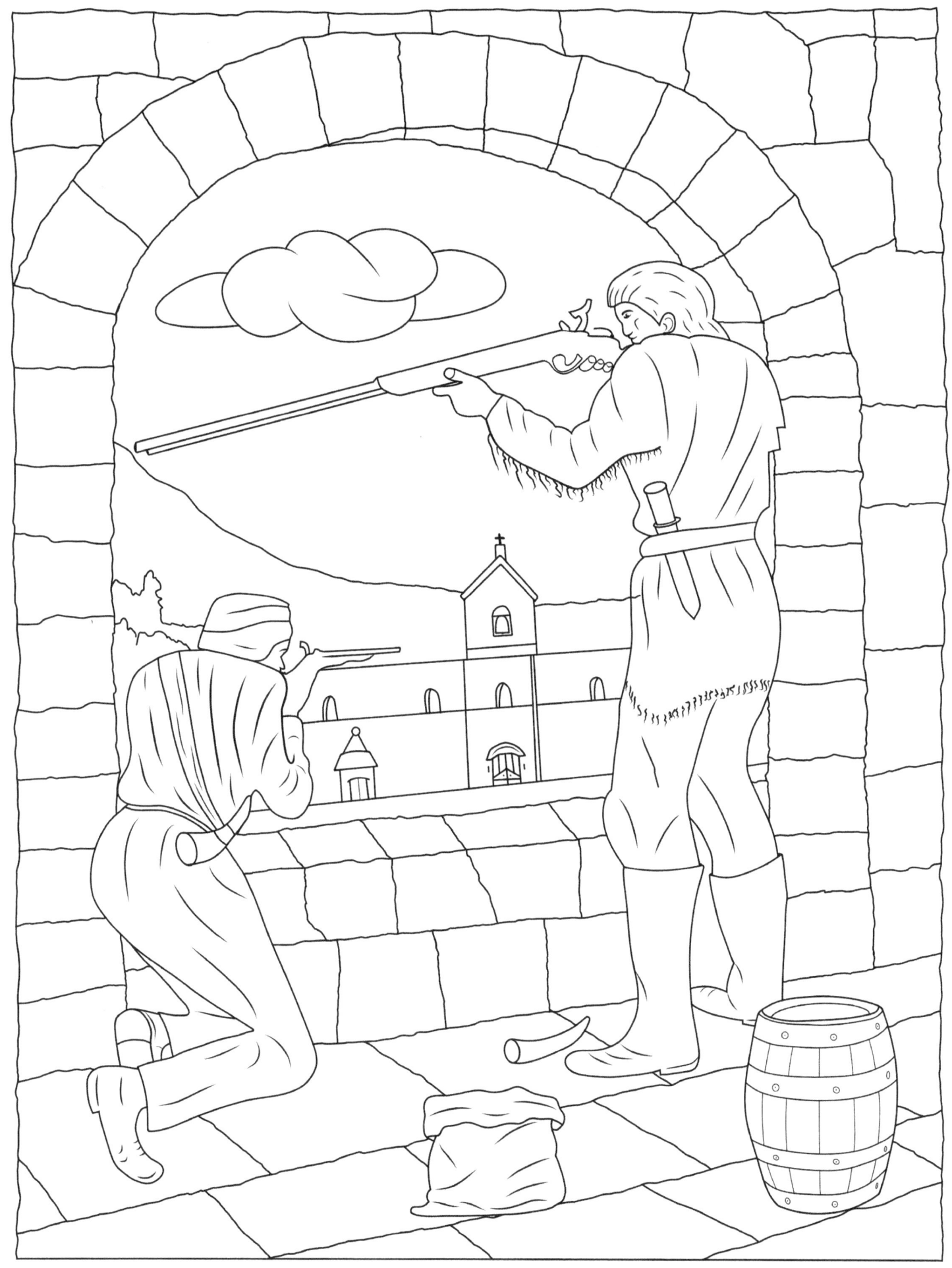

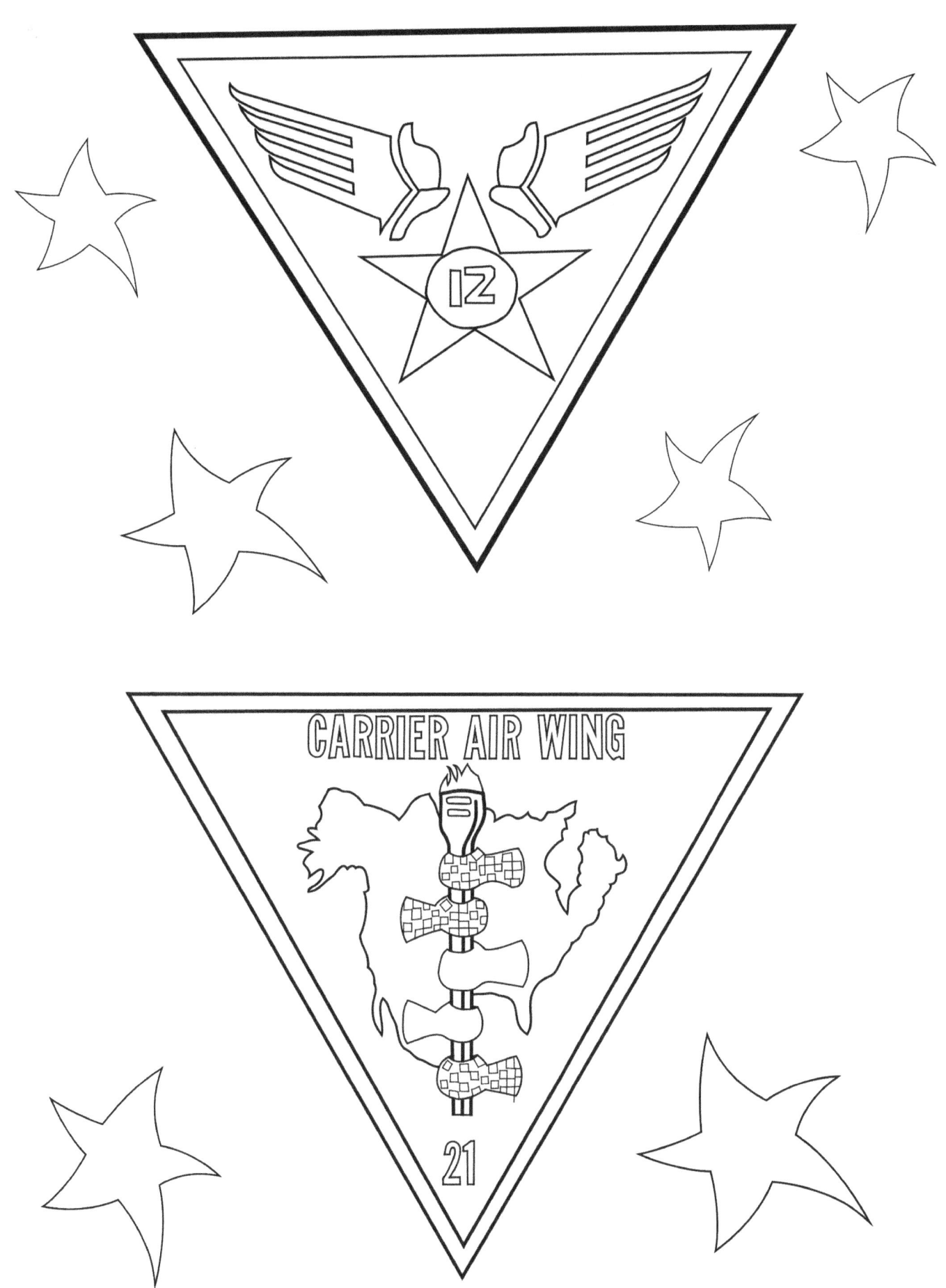

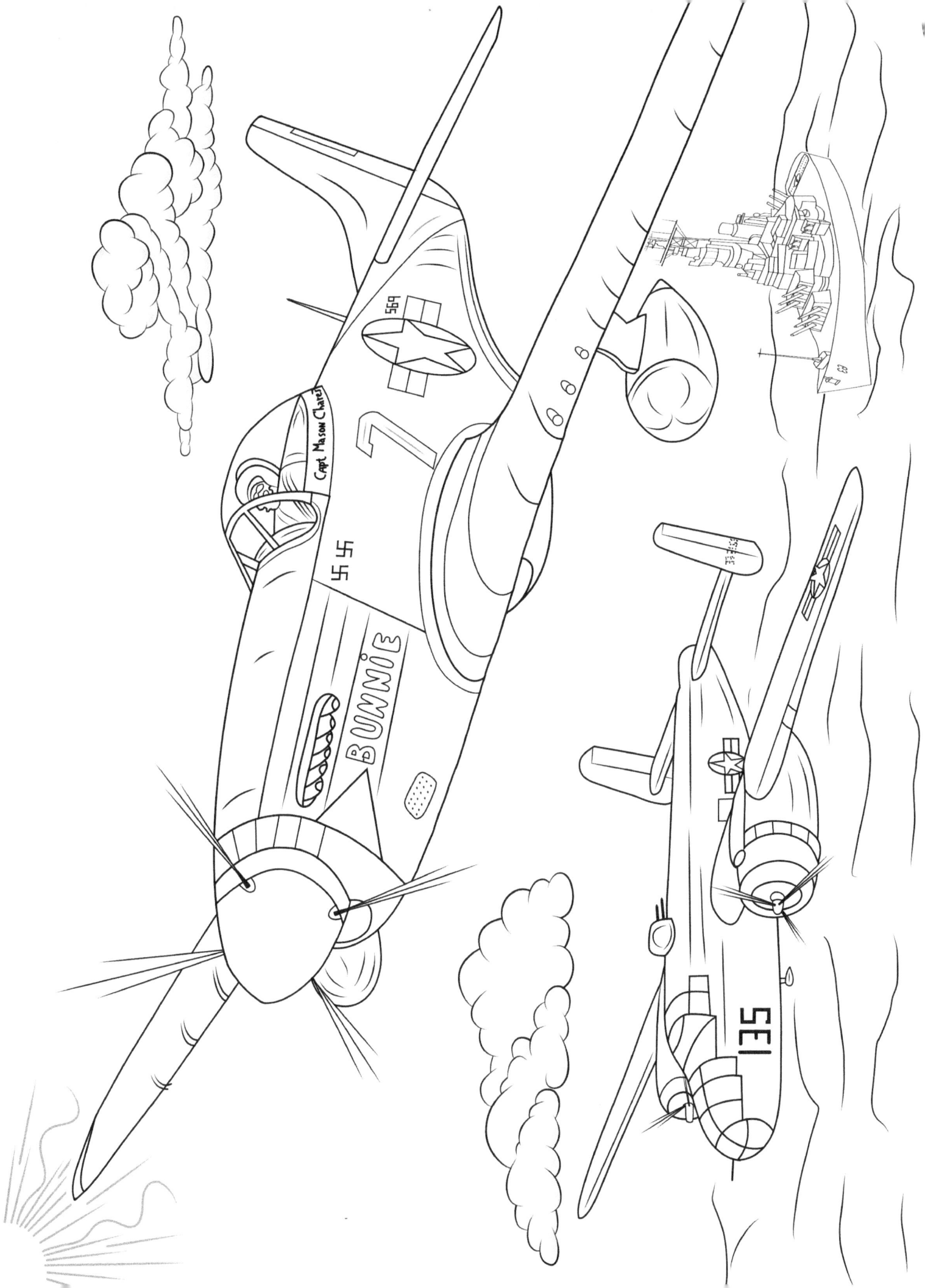

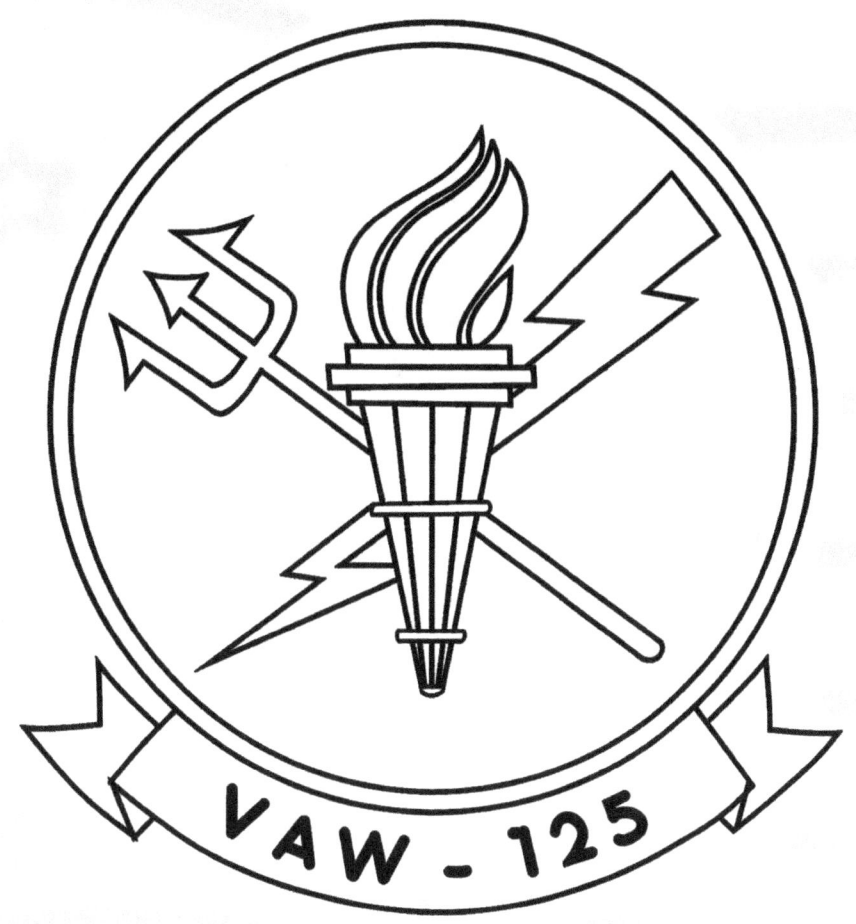

VAW - 125

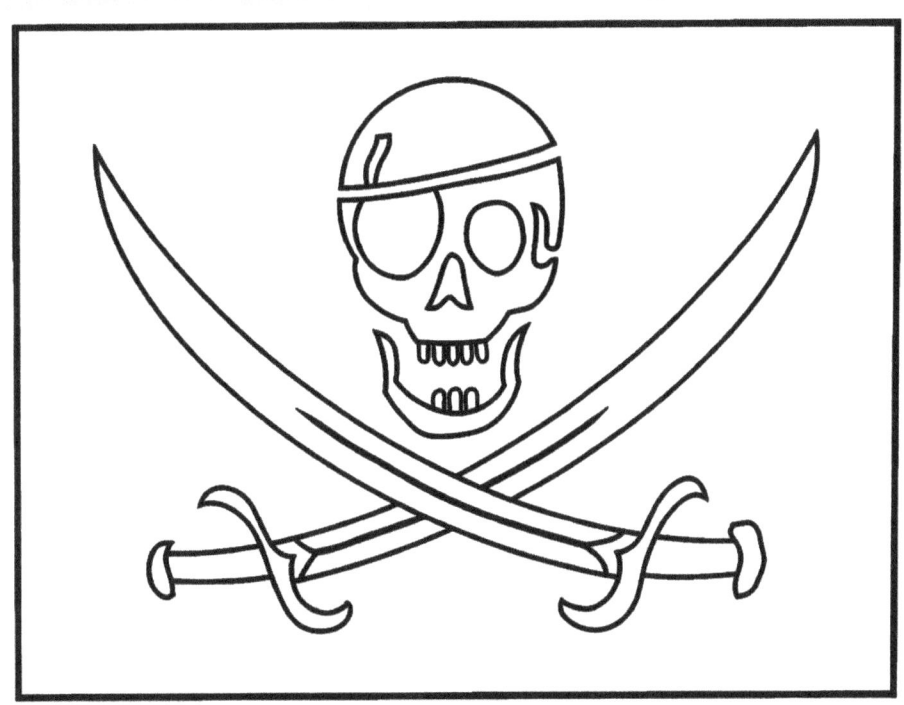

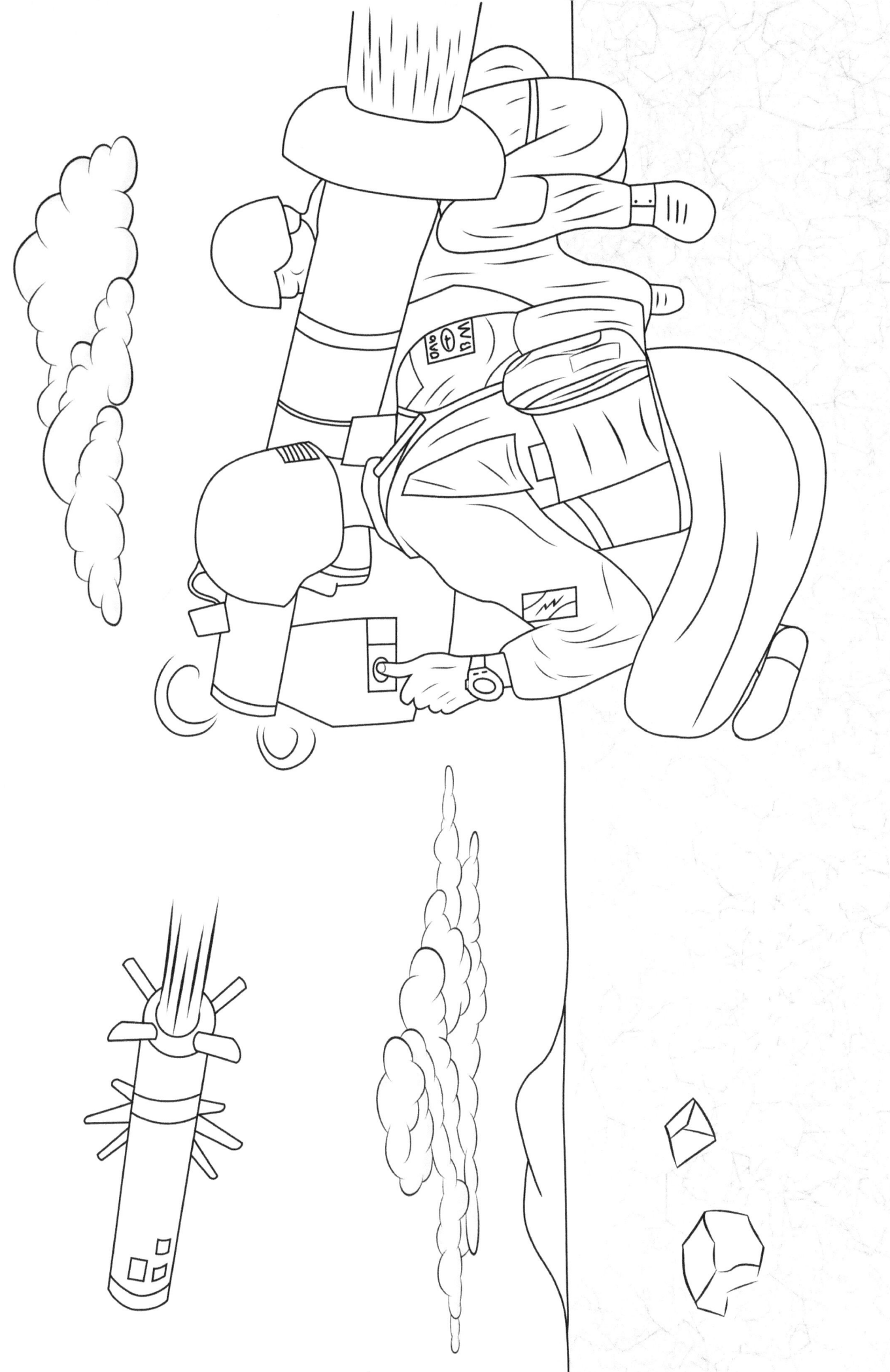

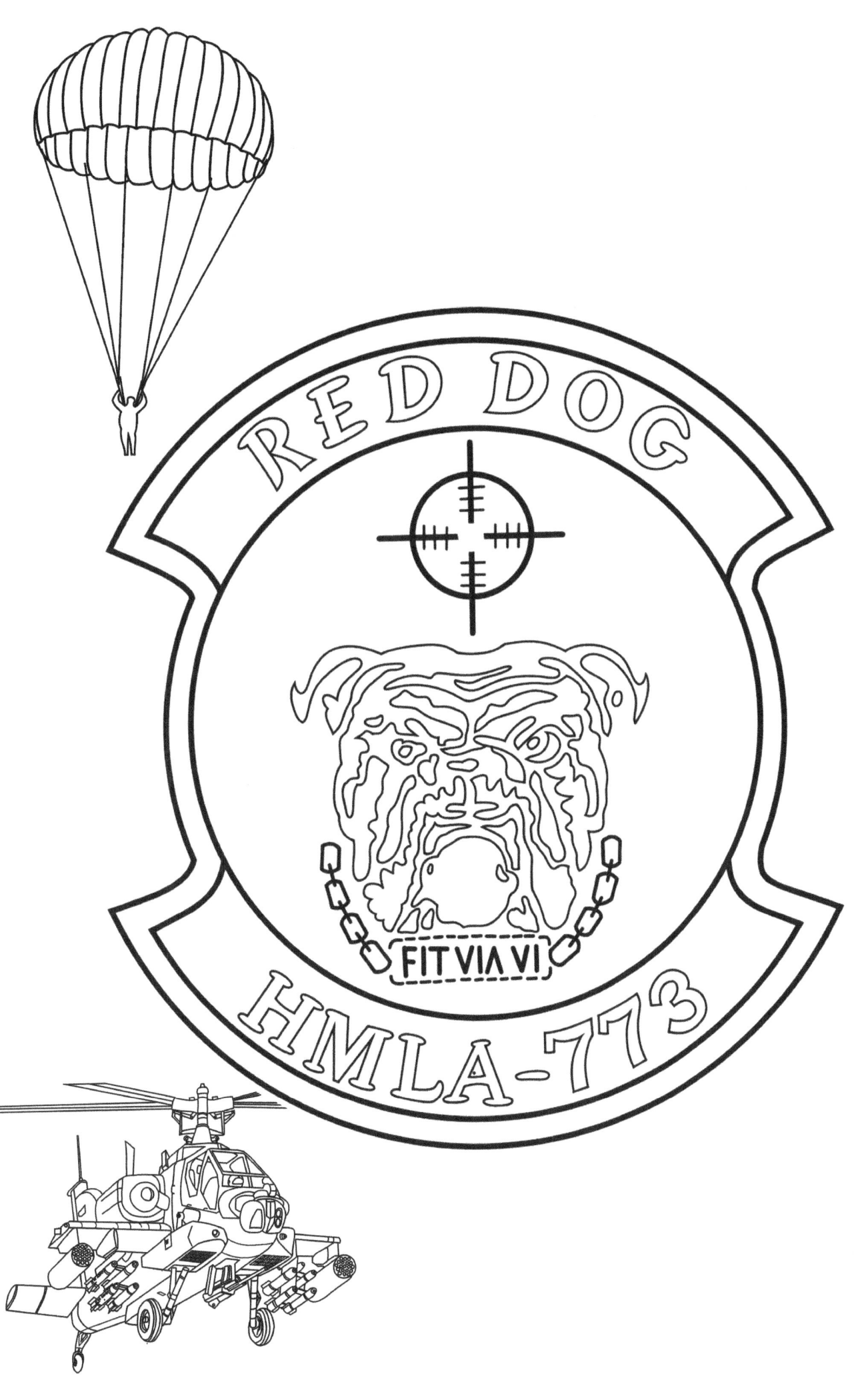

www.ingramcontent.com/pod-product-compliance
Lightning Source LLC
Chambersburg PA
CBHW082216290526
45794CB00009B/3561